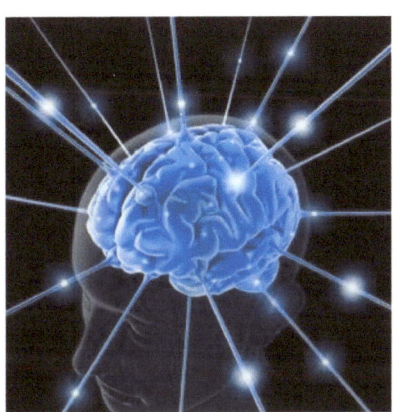

Living with Bipolar II, and Anxiety Disorder.

Don't project your past to the future if the pass experience don't increase your present happiness. The outcome always be a Failure.

By: Luis Mauricio Crespo Falco

10/30/2016

Introduction

Your emotional control start falling apart. I mean any feeling causes pain. There is an intense fear. You feel fear inside & out your body from hands to everyplace. You start getting palpitations, pounding heart, and accelerated heart rate. Then you feel sweating; trembling and shaking; then are sensations of shortness of breath, and choking. At this point you start thinking in your overwhelmed brain what is going on. Nothing can't stop this? God please help me.

Soon you feel paralyzed in bed if you home, or in your car, or at work in some place; you just want to cry. You start praying for help; but no one is there. Your anxiety is wining; then sometimes you also feel down from one day to other; and sometimes from hour to next. The drop off motivation start. You are in depression. You want to sleep; but you can't. Then you get tired and feel like your nervous system is untoned; and you star losing your mental & physical strength. You get sad and lost, and then everything is black. You want to died, but you scare. You ask yourself if you want to continue living like this.....You want help, but who will understand....your brain is controlling you...saying you dying....The rest is history....Welcome to the painfull moments a Bipolar II person combine with an anxiety disorder live.

This book is for those ones that suffer of anxiety and/or bipolar disorder; or someone which have a love one with this mental disorder(s).

The good thing is that hope is there, and this is what I'm looking for the reader to understand. There is real help out there and you must find it. You can live a good quality of life with Bipolar and/or Anxiety.

Discovering Bipolar II Comorbid with Anxiety Disorder.

I remember those terrible emotional moments that start close to when I was 16 years old. I started feeling what today my doctors and I recognize as severe anxiety, with Bipolar II. For me there was not really a name or label for my emotional and physical reactions; it felt simple as the most pain I could ever handle. I was really sick with severe anxiety, and up and down of depression moods. I didn't even knew what anxiety was, and less Bipolar? Probably you the reader are/were in the same spot with your situation or the situation of a love one.

I have my first formal girlfriend which I met in a party of one of my best friends during this time of my life. I really did not felt much passion as I expected for a real first love, or romance; but she was nice and a good girl and I continue the relationship thinking I could fall in love. Well the anxiety trigger on me few weeks later. Somehow I was expected much more of what at that time I understood as Romance Love. I let the relationship go too far and I hide those anxiety moments with depression. I cry, suffer, and finally got depressed and I finish the relationship. I felt horrible that I needed to let her know I was not feeling well with the relationship. I did not know how to handle the situation and I panic. I decide to talk to her and try to explain what was happening. As soon as I stopped the relationship, and said the true to her my anxiety started going away. Surprise...This experience somehow start force on me to think that I probably have a problem when I have close emotional relationships. I have two or three girlfriends before but was nothing serious; I took this as very serious one...I ask myself why?....why so difficult for me ?...why these terrible feelings now called critical anxiety and depression. Or better Bipolar II with Anxiety......I had good moments with her; but the anxiety really win this time.

Anxiety and Bipolar affect relationship specially those when romance is involve. The insecurities anxiety give to your brain can and will affect precious moments into a full thinking of insecurities like having terror the love will go away, trusting yourself feelings, trusted her feelings, etc. If you have Anxiety I recommend to fight in order to have future good relationships.

If I recall correctly, I always was a very passionate kid, and emotional. Very active and full of ideas. I was very creative especially with computers and electronic. Nothing wrong with that; I was a normal kid. But, I remember cry easily for happiness or sad with normal emotions at family or friends level. I cry pretty much always when watching drama or romantic movies, slow music, missing mama & dad when I was away with my friends or other members of family. I was aware very close of my feelings at a very early age. This start since probably at age 4 and never stopped. I remember feeling nervous and great discomfort when friends at school for example call me names, want a fight, or want me to force to be a boyfriend of a girl that I did not like, or do some bad stuff I was not comfortable. Small things like that cause me to feel too much emotional & stress...more than the average Kid.......

After the episode when I was 17 years old, I continue my studies in Electrical engineering and was doing great. These years were 1988 to 1992. I concentrate in my sports and studies 100%. I ran 800 meters and 1500 meters track having the record for the university for long time. I was the best runner for those distances in my college USB (Universidad Simon Bolivar) in Caracas, Venezuela. I compete Nationals and I got some good places. I never was the best in my country; but I was there. I never made the times to go international; but honestly it was good enough. I was an excellent student also, and that help me to recover for my small depression to don't go international. I finish my degree when I was 21 in February 1992. I was isolate in my studies, and sport for long time. Few times I felt anxiety and/or depressed. I had some romance relationships; but nothing serious.

In 1992 surprise again.....close to my graduation I meet someone at the University and we start dating at the end of my degree. She was studding still and needed two more years to finish her degree In Computer Science. Nice girl; but again even I like her and have some good times; I did not feel that romantic or click...This relationship did not went too far; but I start learning something...my anxiety was very severe and increase when I start thinking in our future...the anxiety could not make me enjoy the present; my anxiety convert the great moments in disaster emotional storms. I needed to do something.

I stop the relationship, but I start studying myself more ...... When analyzing I remember that what I feel is the fear to fail in a relationship and that trigger anxiety and later depression...This time the feeling were worse even I stooped the relationship. The worse started for me. I felt so bad, sad, depressed and the anxiety did not stop. I start question myself that I have a terrible problem, something that somehow I could not control much or not at all....I had dough of everything, my feelings, her feelings, life, work, my brain, love, everything... I was worry about what will be the future, I see a bad ending without having any signals.... My anxiety went so bad that I start feelings it was time for help...medical help... I could not eat, sleep, rest, stop thinking, plus all the horrible symptoms that a bad anxiety and depression make you feel.

I did not know much about psychology or phyquiatry, but I went to a therapist. She said I had some issues with becoming a man, but that I had some depression. She give me Prozac.... Oh my God....what a mistake.... Why? Well, Prozac is a SSRI (Selective serotonin re-uptake inhibitors or serotonin-specific reuptake inhibitors). This mean as we that Prozac increase Serotonin in the brain which help with depression. Too little serotonin cause disorders like major depression, obsessive-compulsive disorder and other ; but the problem is that it takes 2 to 4 weeks in average to really start working, but common side effects of Prozac include anxiety before these weeks. So my anxiety went to the worse.

I had the worse reaction from Prozac.... I call my best friend from home and I said that I could not live like this anymore. Internally I was thinking to end this suffering. I can't tell if I was thinking in killing myself, but what I remember is that I was ready to do anything to stop the pain. Prozac increase my anxiety inducing panic attacks, and I needed to be hospitalize. My mother, Father and my all close family agree and drive me directly to one of the best doctors in Venezuela; As soon as he saw me he said "No worries Mauricio; but we need to go now to the hospital, and we will help you there"... I was sent to impatient hospitalization where they applied two ECT (Electro Compulsive Therapy) plus IV Valium. I was diagnose at that time with just Major Depression. Never was mention the word Bipolar I or II or Anxiety Disorder.

After hospitalization the depression got better, but my anxiety was a sleeping monster. MAO and Clonazepam help me a lot but not for strong anxious moments...I only knew that under severity anxiety I always cry in my knees for days. Thanks Mom and dad & close people that encourage me.

Hospitalizations in mental help are very different because is more emotional or traumatic especially when you aware that you sick in the brain. The moment the psych-unit doors locked, You are no longer a sport guy, engineer, son ; you are patient, in a room number and diagnosis. I was told when to sleep and when to wake, when to eat and when to go to group. The routine, now revolved around the clattering sounds of the food trays being brought three times each day from the service elevators into our unit.

Nurses jotted down their observations; my scribbled lines in art therapy were inspected. Everything was scrutinized — except the transformation of my self and my experience of its loss.

When I started working in Venezuela as a professional engineer my anxiety got better but I was always worry so much all the time adapting to a new people and environment...I did lots of sport and I think this and medication make my anxiety decline. I start doing triathlon at national level for 3-4 years. Benzos as I said before (Klonopin / 0.5 mg) help in the bad anxieties...depression was not a problem anymore......but even I was calm several times.....; always anything get me into my worries...that something bad will terminate my job, get nervous in presentations, etc.. But I also remember have hypomanic episodes. I can recall how dedicated and strong I was in my Job tasks and also sports. It was for me normal; but now I can recognize that I was somehow high...I compete in triathlons and wanted to be professional but the times were so hard. I got somehow close again and never compete for Venezuela

International. …Some of my good friends including training partners they became pro and compete in Pan-American Games and Olympics.

For me at that time it was a really a big question of Why I was like this? …In my bad days I ask God several times why this terrible pain; emotional and physical in those moments…….but; I learn how to live and enjoy in my god times. This is something you really learn if you strong enough to pass the bad times…the good times are a gift from God. Lived.

In 1994 I decide to move to USA to improve English…. I ended living here and there are several histories to tell. I was/feel alone many times. I have both great times and also times when my condition made me think how I did it. I always been very strong physical and emotional, but this was hard… There is no pain I can compare when you are in the bad times when bipolar II trigger, and so anxiety.

After all these years from 21 years old until now I have been able to control better my condition; but not more than 65%..I'm consider surgery. We talk about this late. I will need 1000+ pages to write about all my ups and downs. In general I'm a really happy man, but I can't tell you how much Bipolar II + Anxiety affected my life. It is hard to live with, but I never surrender. I know that all I have is a chemical imbalance in my brain. I change many things in my life to feel better and finding the best doctors & medication. I want you the reader use this book and take some positive things to help you understand your condition or the love one and minimize the Stigma created by society.

Another interesting thing I did not long ago was a Genetic test that use you saliva to get your DNA and research your Genes in charge of psychotropic issues. Is interesting to find out that Serotonin Transporter SLC6A4 Gene has issues and is not well responding to SSRIs because is have to do with the presynaptic transmembrane protein responsible for serotonin reuptake…this is amazing. Science is saying that some doctors and researchers are right and I suffer 100% of a genetic disorder and not by any ways something developed by my life experience or environment. This is when we need to focus. Not everyone is the same and environment and life affect for worse or better but mental disorder are genetic period. I have some other genes that are not working properly but I will stop here because we can become too technical that the reader(s) you will say please stop and lets go to the main points. We know that science is there please use it. At the time I publish this small book for sure there will be many other helps for everyone. Please use it. Break the Stigma.

As an impatient with several (Hospitalizations) and outpatient my Journal with mental disorder continue for years, and the war have been always there. I have great support from family and few friends & doctors. I won't lost the war; but yes I been defeated in many battles. Now in my 45 years and a life to live for me and close ones. Stay with me readers. Please never surrender. Mental Health is getting better for all.

Enough about me; let's start talking about important topics about these Mental Disorder(s).

What is Bipolar II and GAD?

First we need to define Bipolar to make clearer our definition. Bipolar is also known as manic depressive illness, where severe and disabling highs (mania), less highs (Hypomania), and lows (depression). In USA 2.2 million Americans are affected. 15% ending their lives in suicide.

Bipolar Disorder is distinguished from Major Depressive Disorder by the presence of manic or hypomanic episodes. Bipolar Disorder is really a spectrum of disorders. Bipolar I disorder is characterized by a history of at least one manic episode, and (usually) depressive episodes. Bipolar II disorder is characterized by hypomanic episodes alternating with depressive episodes (This is what I have). Cyclothymia is characterized by highs which fulfil some but not all criteria for hypomania and lows which fulfil some but not all criteria for depression.

Symptoms during hypomanic episodes include:

- Flying suddenly from one idea to the next
- Having exaggerated self confidence
- Rapid, "pressured" (uninterruptable) and loud speech
- Increased energy, with hyperactivity and a decreased need for sleep
People experiencing hypomanic episodes are often quite pleasant to be around. They can often seem like the "life of the party" -- making jokes, taking an intense interest in other people and activities, and infecting others with their positive mood. The problem is that Hypomania can also lead to erratic and unhealthy behavior. Hypomanic episodes can sometimes progress onward to full manias that affect a person's ability to function (bipolar I disorder). In mania, people might spend money they don't have, seek out sex with people they normally wouldn't, and engage in other impulsive or risky behaviors with the potential for dangerous consequences.

Anxiety can be a symptom of bipolar disorder. This was recognized by the fellow who originally described bipolar disorder as such, Dr. Emil Kraepelin, back in 1921. He described "anxious mania", and also "excited depression", which included a "great restlessness". He specifically named anxiety as one of the components of this illness. All that requires saying, because "anxiety" is not generally regarded as a bipolar symptom.

Yet it clearly is, as summarized in an excellent review by Freeman, Freeman and McElroy.

The International Society for Bipolar Disorders (ISBD) further strengthened the view that anxiety can be part of bipolar disorder in a Task Force. They wrote one particular report deserves attention here: first, because the authors are very well-regarded bipolar experts. Second, because it was published in a top psychiatric journal. And most importantly, because their statements are firm and clear.

General hyper-arousal, Inner tension, Irritability/impatience, Agitation and "Frantically anxious" can be part of bipolar disorder. That ought to be enough to put to rest any controversy about this.

There then two ways to have anxiety with bipolar disorder; First, it can be a symptom of the bipolar disorder itself. Secondly, you can have a separate anxiety condition in addition to bipolar disorder. In medical lingo, that is called a "co-morbid" condition (in case you run across that term). It means both conditions are present, and thus implies that anxiety is a separate condition, not coming from the bipolar disorder itself.

These two ways of looking at anxiety have important implications. If the symptoms are coming from bipolar disorder itself, then they should get better when the bipolar disorder gets better. But if they are coming from a separate condition, they could persist even when the bipolar disorder improves.

If your anxiety is really a separate condition, it's going to require a separate treatment. And that really complicates things, because very often the recommended treatment for the anxiety condition could be an antidepressant medication — and antidepressant medications can make bipolar disorder worse.

Anxiety as a symptom of Bipolar Disorder patients describe it as "agitation", and sometimes that is quite obvious: their foot bounces on the floor while we talk; they pick at their nails; sometimes they can't even bear to sit still and will get up and pace around the office during our interview. But sometimes the agitation is only "inside": patients experience "too much energy inside my skin", like they're going to "explode", and usually their thoughts are going very fast (sometimes called "racing thoughts"). However, when this is severe, people may not experience that fast thinking, but instead just an extremely disorganized thinking — not being able to keep their mind on one thing for more than a few seconds, not being able to accomplish anything. Of course that can make "anxiety" worse as people recognize that they are really ill with something that is not obvious to anyone else, yet they are not really functioning either. How do you explain that to someone?

When this kind of anxiety is present with other manic symptoms like irritability, it can create an awful experience people feel desperate to get out of. (Very often they discover that alcohol can help settle this down for an hour or two. Unfortunately when it wears off, the symptoms come back, very often worse than before. If a person responds to that by drinking more, that can cause a worsening of the condition over several days or weeks

— but because they get brief relief from drinking, they keep doing it and often have to drink more over time to keep their symptoms controlled. This is a dangerous spiral which is statistically associated with successful suicide attempts, so represents a clear reason to get help as soon as possible.) Fortunately there are very good medication approaches to this which can help within an hour.

When this kind of anxiety is present with depression, this may be the worst combination of all. Anxiety is a very strong risk factor for suicide when people are depressed. The future looks hopeless and pointless because of the depression; and the present feels unbearable.

Generalized Anxiety Disorder (GAD) if what will discuss in this book; but we need to remember there are others like Social Phobia, Panic Disorder (with or without Agoraphobia), Post-Traumatic Stress Disorder (PTSD), Obsessive-Compulsive Disorder (OCD), Specific Phobias, etc.

There is a lot of overlap in the diagnostic criteria for GAD and bipolar II. We need to look at this in some detail because they may be actually the same thing, at least in some people (as opposed to the rest of the list below, which are somewhat more "separate").

Generalized anxiety disorder is characterized by persistent, excessive, and unrealistic worry about everyday things. People with the disorder, experience excessive anxiety and worry, often expecting the worst even when there is no apparent reason for concern. They anticipate disaster and may be overly concerned about money, health, family, work, or other issues. GAD is diagnosed when a person finds it difficult to control worry on more days than not for at least six months and has three or more symptoms.

Sometimes just the thought of getting through the day produces anxiety. They don't know how to stop the worry cycle and feel it is beyond their control, even though they usually realize that their anxiety is more intense than the situation warrants. The disorder comes on gradually and can begin across the life cycle, though the risk is highest between childhood and middle age. Although the exact cause of GAD is unknown, there is evidence that biological factors, family background, and life experiences, particularly stressful ones, play a role.

When their anxiety level is mild, people with GAD can function socially and be gainfully employed. Although they may avoid some situations because they have the disorder, some people can have difficulty carrying out the simplest daily activities when their anxiety is severe.

History about Anxiety

A century ago, Freud noted that chronic, free-floating anxiety occurred frequently in the general population, and yet, to this day, there is limited information available about the natural history of this disorder. Its resemblance to normal anxiety and the lack of distinctive distinguishing features have led to poor diagnostic reliability and questions about the validity of the disorder. The relative mildness of the symptoms and the high rate of comorbidity with other psychiatric disorders--the highest of all the anxiety disorders--have caused some to view it as an associated feature of a number of other disorders rather than as an independent disturbance. Nevertheless, no matter where the diagnostic threshold is set, GAD is common, and it is the least studied of the anxiety disorders.

A major change in the nosology of anxiety disorders occurred in 1980, when changes in classification adopted by the American Psychiatric Association (APA) separated anxiety neurosis (DSM-II) into panic disorder, characterized by spontaneous episodes of intense anxiety, and GAD, a residual category for patients who have chronic, sustained anxiety without panic attacks (DSM-III). The distinction between these 2 disorders was defended at the time by the observation of a differential response to medication. Klein noted that panic disorder responded to imipramine while GAD responded best to benzodiazepines (although it has been demonstrated more recently that patients with GAD also respond to imipramine as well as or better than to benzodiazepines if taken for a sufficient length of time). In DSM-III, hierarchical rules prohibited the diagnosis of GAD if another psychiatric disorder was comorbid with the chronic anxiety symptoms.

In DSM-III-R, GAD was given independent status, with clearly defined symptom criteria. The trait of excessive worry was identified as the core symptom of GAD. With the revised classification, most hierarchical rules were eliminated, making it possible for patients to meet criteria for GAD and other anxiety or depressive disorders simultaneously.

The changes in diagnostic criteria from DSM-III to DSM-IV are base on modified the symptom checklist to reflect symptoms that best discriminate between normal and pathologic anxiety. The essential feature of GAD is excessive or pathologic worry. Although subjects with GAD may not be able to identify their worrying as excessive, they do report that the constancy of this feeling causes them distress, is difficult to control, and has an impact on their life secondary to the objects of their worry. Among a number of population studies using various diagnostic criteria, estimates of the lifetime prevalence of GAD have ranged between 4.0% and 6.6%.

Perhaps the best epidemiologic data on GAD come from one of these reports, which was based on data collected in the National Comorbidity Survey (NCS).The NCS was a general population survey of noninstitutionalized American civilians 15 to 54 years of age. The study was quite large (N=8098) and utilized the most current DSM-III-R criteria available at that time. The results were reported with and without diagnostic hierarchical rules. In the absence of such exclusions, the prevalence of GAD in the total sample was 1.6% for current GAD (defined as a 6-month period of anxiety that continued in the 30 days prior to the interview), 3.1% for GAD within the previous 12-month period, and 5.1% for lifetime GAD. Regardless of the time frame, there was a clear predominance of women with GAD, with a 2:1 female/male ratio. The prevalence was lowest in the youngest age group and increased with age: The prevalence in women aged 45 and older was 3.5% for those with current GAD and 10.3% for lifetime occurrence of GAD. Prevalence estimates did not change significantly when diagnostic hierarchical rules were imposed to exclude respondents whose GAD occurred exclusively during episodes of a mood or psychotic disorder--only 8% of subjects with GAD reported symptoms exclusively during episodes of another disorder. The researchers found that homemakers and unemployed respondents (mostly permanently disabled individuals and early retirees) had a significantly higher prevalence of GAD than other subjects.

There was a significant regional difference in GAD as well, with a higher lifetime prevalence in the Northeast than in other parts of the country. Predictors that were not found to be significant in this study included education, marital status, and urbanicity. Importantly, the researchers investigated potential differences between patients without psychiatric comorbidity (ie, primary GAD--in patients with an earlier onset of GAD compared with their comorbid psychiatric disorder) and secondary GAD (ie, a later age of GAD onset than the comorbid psychiatric disorder).They found no differences between these groups with regard to age, sex, race, or social class, lending validity to the independent status of GAD.

Noyes and colleagues reported a study of GAD and panic disorder in a treatment-seeking population and found significant differences between the groups. They found that patients with GAD had a significantly earlier age of onset, as well as more psychologic symptoms and fewer physiologic symptoms than patients with panic disorder. The GAD subjects were older at the time that they sought treatment, and fewer had been treated in the past. The investigators noted significant comorbidity with psychiatric disorders, and the patterns were different from those seen in the panic-disorder patients. The authors of this article noted that, while the study supported a distinction between the 2 disorders as well as diagnostic validity for GAD, the importance of GAD may not be so much the disorder itself as its tendency to accompany other disorders.

In psychiatry, where few biologic markers for disease exist, family and follow-up studies provide the scientific infrastructure for diagnosis and classification. Familial transmission is a strong validator of psychiatric syndromes. Schizophrenia and bipolar spectrum disorders provide good examples of this principle. Studies of families have shown that these illnesses breed true--that probands with one illness have increased numbers of relatives with that illness, but not with other psychiatric disorders.[Family studies can also determine whether subsyndromal cases of a disorder are transmitted familiarly. In this way, family studies can provide validation of the existence of disease entities and contribute to defining their diagnostic boundaries. The importance of diagnosis and classification has taken on new meaning in the era of molecular genetics, because in order to succeed, strategies that aim to find disease genes require biologically valid phenotypes.

Family studies of the individual anxiety disorders have found that there is an elevated risk of the index anxiety disorder in first-degree relatives, but that other anxiety disorders are not increased. These studies, however, have been done using clinical populations and probands with only one disorder.

Two studies have examined the transmission of GAD in families. They both used clinic populations of probands without comorbid illness, and looked at the transmission of more than one type of anxiety disorder. Noyes and colleagues compared first-degree relatives of 20 probands with GAD, 20 with panic disorder without agoraphobia, 20 with agoraphobia, and 20 controls. They found that each disorder was transmitted to relatives at a significantly higher rate and that other anxiety disorders were not, indicating that there is a distinction between the 3 disorders and that there may be a genetic component to the illness.

Mendelwitz and associates compared the first-degree relatives of 25 probands with panic disorder without agoraphobia, 25 with GAD, 25 with major depressive disorder (MDD), and 25 normal controls. Unfortunately, the panic disorder probands were diagnosed using the Structured Clinical Interview for DSM-III (SCID) and DSM-III criteria, whereas the GAD and major depressive disorder probands were diagnosed using the Schedule for Affective Disorders and Schizophrenia (SADS-LA) and Research Diagnostic Criteria (RDC). The correlation between instruments is not well established, and the impact that it had on this study is not known. This study found that the relatives of panic disorder probands had panic disorder at rates significantly higher than the relatives of GAD, MDD, and control probands, and that they did not have higher rates of GAD, MDD, or agoraphobia. They did not find an elevated risk of GAD in the relatives of GAD probands or of MDD in the relatives of MDD probands, in contrast to previous family studies. Table III summarizes the available data from family studies of anxiety disorders.

Twin studies of anxiety disorders have, for the most part, been general-population studies, and probands may have had more than 1 anxiety disorder diagnosis as well as major depression. While this is more representative of how these disorders occur in clinical populations as well as in the general population, these studies have not been easy to reconcile. Slater and Shields reported on a twin study of anxiety neurosis which found that 7 of 17 monozygotic (MZ, "identical") twin pairs (41%) were concordant for anxiety neurosis, compared with 1 of 28 dizygotic (DZ, "fraternal") pairs (4%). The study by Torgersen of anxiety in twins was gathered from a nationwide study in Norway of adult same-sex twins who had been treated for a psychiatric disorder in the 1970s. Torgersen found no difference in concordance between MZ and DZ twins for GAD, but the number of affected twins was small in this study.

In a larger study, Andrews and coworkers evaluated anxiety disorders in 446 pairs of same-sex and opposite-sex twins from the Australian twin registry. The mean age and the sex distribution were not reported. The investigators found a concordance rate for GAD of 21.5% (13/63 twin pairs) in MZ twins, compared with a 13.5% (11/81) concordance rate in DZ twins. The differences were not statistically significant, but the numbers were small, and, in contrast to Torgersen's findings, the trend in this study was towards a greater concordance for GAD among MZ twins than DZ twins. Similarly, Kendler and associates examined 1033 same-sex female twin pairs from the Virginia twin registry and found statistically significant evidence for a genetic effect in GAD. However, they did not use DSM-III or DSM-IV criteria exclusively--they used 9 different sets of diagnostic criteria, searching for the criteria that revealed the largest genetic effect. For example, they found that a 1-month duration criterion, which was used as the duration criterion in DSM-III, was more heritable than the 6-month duration criterion used in DSM-III-R and DSM-IV. This study did evaluate comorbid diagnoses and found that GAD was heritable regardless of comorbid anxiety disorders or depression.

The twin studies, like the family studies, do not agree on the heritability of GAD. The larger studies have found a greater genetic contribution, but there is clearly an environmental component as well. Studying adoptees who were separated from their biological families at birth and reared by adoptive families is an excellent method of evaluating genetic and environmental influences independent of one another. Unfortunately, there have not been any adoption studies of anxiety disorders. It is difficult to do adoption studies for chronic but less incapacitating illnesses, such as anxiety disorders, where patients are infrequently hospitalized and reliable data are harder to obtain. In the absence of a genetic marker for GAD, we are left with family and twin studies. A likely explanation of the differences in findings between these studies is that when genetic effects are modest, as they appear to be with GAD, larger samples and more severely ill samples are required to identify them.

Barlow speculated that GAD was a more chronic and severe disorder than panic disorder. He hypothesized that GAD, with its earlier age of onset, longer course, and less robust response to treatment than other anxiety disorders, could cause greater disruption in subjects' lives than other anxiety disorders. Unfortunately, few studies have examined the course of GAD and patients' response to treatment. Follow-up studies done prior to 1980 are problematic, because it is unclear what percentage of the patients had GAD versus panic disorder. It is assumed that, using current criteria, a majority of patients in these studies would be diagnosed with panic disorder, because most studies used treatment-seeking populations, and these populations are inclined to have more severe illness. Therefore, conclusions about the nature of GAD gathered from these studies should be made cautiously.

A number of GAD follow-up studies completed after 1980 fulfill the minimum criteria for validity as outlined by Greer in 1969: (a) an unselected series of patients with anxiety states followed up after at least 1 year; (b) outcome ascertained in at least 75% of the original sample; and © follow-up information obtained by personal interview. The information gathered from these studies demonstrated, for the most part, that anxiety disorders have a chronic, fluctuating course. Although some patients experience exacerbations and remissions, the percentage is low. In one follow-up investigation, 24% of anxious medical patients reported symptom-free intervals, but only 12% were symptom-free at the time they were reinterviewed. While full recovery is unusual, roughly 50% of patients were improved at follow-up. One study found lower socioeconomic status associated with poorer outcome.

The 1-year follow-up data from the Environmental Catchment Area (ECA) study, done in 1980, found that the recovery rate for GAD (defined as no longer meeting criteria for GAD, rather than being free of symptoms) was 56%.This figure--the second highest reported in this study for any psychiatric disorders--is hard to evaluate, because poorly defined criteria were used (DSM-III), and coexisting disorders were not excluded and not taken into account. Nevertheless, data from the ECA study suggest that GAD may last for decades, if not a lifetime, in many patients.Unfortunately, GAD was diagnosed at only 3 of the 5 sites involved in the study, but data from these sites revealed an average duration of illness between 6.5 and 10.4 years. Indeed, 40% of patients reported the presence of symptoms for more than 5 years, and more than 10% had symptoms for longer than 20 years. Although the researchers noted that the onset of GAD could occur at any time during life, more than 35% of patients with panic disorder or phobia in the same study dated the onset of "being a nervous person" at age 10 or younger, which suggests that excessive worry and anxiety in patients with anxiety disorders may begin in childhood and eventually reach syndromal levels many years later, perhaps due to inevitable role changes and stresses during life.

Mancuso and associates followed up with 50 patients 16 months after initial evaluation. They reinterviewed 88% of probands and found that 50% had remitted and 50% met criteria for GAD. They found that no patients developed disorders that they had not had at baseline during the follow-up period. This study lends limited support to the diagnostic classification of GAD, but only limited conclusions can be drawn from these data because the researchers did not attempt to quantify persistent symptoms in probands who did or did not meet criteria for GAD.

Rickels and colleagues reviewed the literature on GAD related to treatment and outcome and found that the available information suggests that GAD has a chronic course, with significant long-term distress and morbidity. They conducted a 40-month follow-up study with patients who met DSM-III-R criteria for GAD. They reinterviewed 75% of patients and found that 58% of the clorazepate-treated group and 25% of the buspirone-treated group reported moderate to severe anxiety symptoms and illustrated, in a prospective manner, the chronic nature of GAD. There was no significant difference in outcomes between the 2 treatment groups.

Woodman and coworkers studied 64 patients with GAD and 68 patients with panic disorder, comparing diagnostic stability and course and outcome of GAD, as contrasted with panic disorder. They were interviewed an average of 5 years (range, 3 to 7 years) after their enrollment in drug treatment studies and were treated naturally thereafter (ie, no structured treatment over follow-up period). At baseline, the GAD group was significantly older and had more education, earlier onset, and longer duration of illness than subjects with panic disorder. GAD subjects also had less severe symptoms, as measured by both clinician-rated and self-rated instruments. At follow-up, there was diagnostic stability for both GAD and panic disorder. Significantly fewer GAD subjects achieved partial or full remission at follow-up (37% vs 63%). On measures of the symptoms and severity of anxiety, GAD probands were not different from panic disorder probands at follow-up.

Although GAD appears to be a less severe disorder than panic disorder at the time that patients seek treatment, it has an earlier onset and a more chronic course than panic disorder. It may also be less responsive to naturalistic treatment. The limited data available related to the course and outcome of GAD clearly distinguish it from panic disorder and support its diagnostic validity.

Pure GAD appears to be relatively rare, and there is significant overlap with normal anxiety or other psychiatric disorders (Fig. 1). The most frequent complications of GAD are comorbid depression, alcohol abuse, and other anxiety disorders. Of particular note is that while only 8% of persons with GAD in this study met criteria only in the midst of another disorder, 90.4% of persons with GAD met criteria for another psychiatric disorder over the course of their lifetime. The most frequently noted concern raised about the validity of the diagnosis of GAD is the fact that it is associated with these high rates of comorbidity, as both a principal diagnosis and a secondary diagnosis.

Several studies have shown that there is diagnostic overlap between GAD and other anxiety disorders. Comorbidity with specific phobia occurs most frequently, but of all the anxiety disorders, panic disorder occurs at a much higher rate than its occurrence in the general population. Woodman and associates followed up patients with panic disorder an average of 5 years after their initial evaluation and found that while 73% had panic disorder in remission, 25% of those in remission still met criteria for GAD.

Major depression has a high rate of comorbidity with anxiety disorders as a group and with GAD specifically. The National Comorbidity Survey found that both major depression and dysthymia occurred together at rates well above what would be expected in the general population. This comorbidity has led to questions of diagnostic validity for GAD, as opposed to a disorder that is a part of depression. Gray and Paul have both proposed specific biologic models to account for the high rates of overlap between chronic anxiety and depression, based largely on the learned-helplessness paradigm. Laboratory animals exposed to repeated noxious stimuli initially demonstrate an increase in arousal (ie, the equivalent of human anxiety), which is followed by behavioral immobility (ie, the equivalent of human depression). Kendler and colleagues found that major depression and GAD traveled together in twins, and they postulated that the 2 disorders might be alternative expressions of the same gene. This is a controversial area, and more research is required to explore possible etiologies of the extensive overlap between the disorders.

Substance use disorders occur frequently in individuals with anxiety disorders, and GAD is no exception. As alcohol is the oldest anxiolytic known to humanity, there has been a long-standing distinction made between patients whose anxiety precedes the onset of alcohol abuse and those who develop an anxiety disorder secondary to alcohol abuse. The former can be seen as an out-of-control attempt to self-medicate the anxiety disorder, whereas the latter can be viewed as secondary to the physiologic consequences of alcohol dependence. In both situations, the initial treatment involves detoxification and psychosocial support, but subsequent treatment can be widely divergent for a primary anxiety disorder, compared with a secondary anxiety disorder.

The overlap between GAD and personality disorder has not been well studied. The early age of onset, modest response to treatment, and chronicity seen in GAD are features shared with personality disorders. The degree of comorbidity between these diagnoses needs further study.

Despite the frequent comorbidity of GAD and other psychiatric disorders, it does not appear to be associated with suicidality. Asnis and colleagues found that in a psychiatric outpatient population, lifetime prevalence of suicidal ideation was 18% and suicide attempts 17% in patients with a diagnosis of GAD. This is significantly lower than the lifetime prevalence seen with MDD, substance use disorders, and even adjustment disorders.

GAD has extensive comorbidity with other psychiatric disorders, and while this has led to some question regarding diagnostic validity, the vast majority of subjects with comorbid disorders meet criteria for GAD in the absence of another diagnosis at some time during the course of their illness.

There are limited data related to the predictors of outcome for anxiety disorders, and GAD is no exception. Furthermore, the prognostic factors identified for anxiety disorders may not apply to GAD. However, the general rule that the future course of the illness is best predicted by the past course almost certainly applies to GAD. This has been confirmed in at least 2 studies (Noyes and associates Woodman and coworkers). Angst and Vollrath found that no demographic factor was of significant prognostic value for anxiety disorders, although occupational status, social class, and marital status were suggested to have some value.

While the significance of comorbidity continues to be controversial as it pertains to the validity of the diagnosis of GAD, the presence of comorbid disorders does appear to have a significant effect on prognosis.Mancuso and associates noted that GAD patients with personality disorders, dysthymia, and social phobia had a worse prognosis than patients without these disorders. Woodman and colleagues found that patients with comorbid MDD had a poorer outcome than those without major depression. Noyes and coworkers[11] noted that individuals with chronic physical disorders had more severe GAD.

Life events also may have an effect on the course of GAD. Some studies have found that stressors and life changes have an unfavorable impact on the prognosis of GAD, but others have found that they have no impact. Kendler and associates noted that more life events were associated with the expression of GAD in a general-population study of female-female twin pairs. This area of research appears fruitful and should be explored further.

There is limited information about the predictors of outcome in individuals with GAD, but the factors identified are similar to those found to predict outcome in other anxiety disorders and depressive disorders. Earlier age of onset, more severe symptoms at the time of diagnosis, and prior treatment are associated with a poorer prognosis. The presence of GAD may predict a worse outcome for subjects with another psychiatric diagnosis; this has been the most important finding related to comorbidity and GAD. The research in the area of outcomes and GAD needs further exploration.

Unfortunately, most GAD patients may never receive treatment. Data from one survey indicated that only about 25% of individuals with GAD ever receive treatment.

There are few follow-up studies of GAD or anxiety neurosis, but the existing ones have shown that GAD is a stable diagnosis. In addition, while comorbidity is common at the time that the subject seeks treatment, additional disorders do not appear to eclipse or obliterate the disorder with the passage of time. These studies have also shown that, in contrast to the remitting course of depressive illnesses, GAD is chronic in treatment-seeking populations. This difference in outcome is critical to differentiating between depressive disorders and anxiety disorders.

Follow-up studies have found that GAD is chronic and has an ongoing impact on occupational and social function. It is not known whether community populations experience a similar chronicity, due to a lack of longitudinal follow-up data in this population. If we assume a spectrum of severity, then we would expect to find milder illness in the community as well as in primary care settings, and milder illness might be more likely to be remitting. Again, there is little information concerning this possibility at present, and further research is needed.

The diagnostic validity of GAD has been questioned since its inception in 1980. Although there is limited information about the course and outcome of this disorder, especially in the elderly and in children, the existing data support GAD as an independent diagnosis. GAD is a chronic and disabling disorder that is stable over time and distinguishable from other anxiety disorders. There are a number of unanswered questions related to this disorder: Future research is needed to delineate the severity of the illness over time as well as effective treatment.

History about Bipolar II

Bipolar disorder is one of the most highly investigated neurological disorders. The National Institute of Mental Health (NIMH) estimates that it affects over 2 percent of adults in the United States. Of these, nearly 83 percent have "severe" cases of the disorder. Unfortunately, due to social stigma, funding issues, and a lack of education, less than 40 percent receive what the NIMH calls "minimally adequate treatment."
The history of bipolar disorder is perhaps just as complex as the condition itself. Bipolar is highly recognized as a treatable disorder. The more we learn about bipolar disorder, the more people may be able to receive the help that they need.

Aretaeus of Cappadocia began the process of detailing symptoms in the medical field as early as the 1st Century in Greece. His notes on the link between mania and depression went largely unnoticed for many centuries.
The ancient Greeks and Romans were responsible for the terms "mania" and "melancholia," which are now the modern day manic and depressive. They even discovered that using lithium salts in baths calmed manic people and lifted the spirits of depressed people. Today, lithium is a common treatment for bipolar patients.

The Greek philosopher Aristotle not only acknowledged melancholy as a condition, but thanked it as the inspiration for the great artists of his time.

It was common during this time for people across the globe to be executed for having bipolar disorder and other mental conditions. As the study of medicine advanced, strict religious dogma stated that these people were possessed by demons and should therefore be put to death.

In the 17th Century, Robert Burton wrote the book, The Anatomy of Melancholy, which addressed the issue of treating melancholy (non-specific depression) using music and dance as a form of treatment. While mixed with medical knowledge, the book primarily serves as a literary collection of commentary on depression, and a vantage point of the full effects of depression on society. It did, however, expand deeply into the symptoms and treatments of what is now known as clinical depression.

Later that century, Theophilus Bonet published a great work titled Sepuchretum, a text that drew from his experience performing 3,000 autopsies. In it, he linked mania and melancholy in a condition called "manico-melancolicus."
This was a substantial step in diagnosing the disorder because mania and depression were most often considered separate disorders.

19th and 20th Century Discoveries Centuries passed and little new was discovered about bipolar disorder until French psychiatrist Jean-Pierre Falret published an article in 1851 describing what he called "la folie circulaire," which translates to circular insanity. The article details people switching through severe depression and manic excitement, and is considered to be the first documented diagnosis of bipolar disorder.

In addition to making the first diagnosis, Falret also noted the genetic connection in bipolar disorder, something medical professionals still believe to this day.

The history of bipolar disorder changed with Emil Kraepelin, a German psychiatrist who broke away from Sigmund Freud's theory that society and the suppression of desires played a large role in mental illness. Kraepelin recognized biological causes of mental illnesses. He is believed to be the first person to seriously study mental illnesses.

Kraepelin's Manic Depressive Insanity and Paranoia in 1921 detailed the difference between manic-depressive and praecox, which is now known as schizophrenia. His classification of mental disorders remains the basis used by professional associations today.
A professional classification system for mental disorders — which was important to better understand and treat conditions — has its earliest roots in the early 1950s from German psychiatrist Karl Leonhard and others.

The term "bipolar" — which means "two poles" signifying the polar opposites of mania and depression—first appeared in the American Psychiatric

Association's (AMA) Diagnostic and Statistical Manual of Mental Disorders (DSM) in its third revision in 1980.
It was that revision that did away with the term mania to avoid calling patients "maniacs." Now in it's fifth version, the DSM is considered the leading manual for mental health professionals.

The current version (DSM-5) lists the following subtypes of bipolar disorder with the following diagnostic criteria:

Bipolar I Disorder
- at least one manic episode and one or more major depression episode
- equally common in men and women, with the first episode in men usually being mania, and the first episode in women typically being major depression.

Bipolar II Disorder
- major depression
- instead of full-on mania, they experience hypomania: high energy, impulsiveness, and excitability, but less severe as full-fledged mania.
- more common in women than men

Cyclothymic Disorder
- less severe mood swings
- episodes shifting from hypomania to mild depression
- rapid changes in mood — with four or more episodes of major depression, mania, hypomania, or mixed symptoms within a year.
- may have more than one episode in a week or even within one day
- more common in people who have their first episode at a younger age
- affects more women than men

Rapid-Cycling Bipolar Disorder
Rapid-cycling bipolar disorder includes the same fluctuations manic and depressive symptoms. The difference is that the cycles are shorter, so people experience shorter, more frequent bursts of manic and depressive posts. This is considered the most severe form of bipolar disorder.

Our understanding of bipolar disorder has certainly evolved since ancient times. Fortunately, great advances in education and treatment have also come a long way in just the past century alone. Still, there is a lot of work to be done because many people aren't getting the treatment they need to lead better quality lives.

While bipolar disorder typically shows up in a person's 20s, it can appear during any stage of life. It's important to identify the symptoms so you can help yourself or a loved one who might have the condition. The earlier a person receives a diagnosis, the more effective a treatment plan may be. Long-term solutions often involve a combination of medications and counseling.

Some Science to help understand Better Bipolar II and Anxiety.

Neurons are the basic working unit of the brain and nervous system. These cells are highly specialized for the function of conducting messages. A neuron has three basic parts:

- **Cell body** which includes the nucleus, cytoplasm, and cell organelles. The nucleus contains DNA and information that the cell needs for growth, metabolism, and repair. Cytoplasm is the substance that fills a cell, including all the chemicals and parts needed for the cell to work properly including small structures called cell organelles.
- **Dendrites** branch off from the cell body and act as a neuron's point of contact for receiving chemical and electrical signals called impulses from neighboring neurons.
- **Axon** which sends impulses and extends from cell bodies to meet and deliver impulses to another nerve cell. Axons can range in length from a fraction of an inch to several feet.

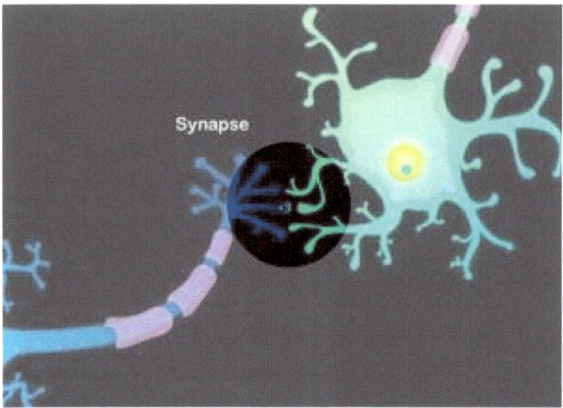

Fig1.

Each neuron is enclosed by a cell membrane, which separates the inside contents of the cell from its surrounding environment and controls what enters and leaves the cell, and responds to signals from the environment; this all helps the cell maintain its balance with the environment.

Synapses are tiny gaps between neurons, where messages move from one neuron to another as chemical or electrical signals.

The brain begins as a small group of cells in the outer layer of a developing embryo. As the cells grow and differentiate, neurons travel from a central "birthplace" to their final destination. Chemical signals from other cells guide neurons in forming various brain structures. Neighboring neurons make connections with each other and with distant nerve cells (via axons) to form brain circuits. These circuits control specific body functions such as sleep and speech.

The brain continues maturing well into a person's early 20s. Knowing how the brain is wired and how the normal brain's structure develops and matures helps scientists understand what goes wrong in mental illnesses.

Scientists have already begun to chart how the brain develops over time in healthy people and are working to compare that with brain development in people mental disorders. Genes and environmental cues both help to direct this growth.

There are many different types of cells in the body. We say that cells differentiate as the embryo develops, becoming more specialized for specific functions. Skin cells protect, muscle cells contract, and neurons, the most highly specialized cells of all, conduct messages.

Every cell in our bodies contains a complete set of DNA. DNA, the "recipe of life," contains all the information inherited from our parents that helps to define who we are, such as our looks and certain abilities, such as a good singing voice. A gene is a segment of DNA that contains codes to make proteins and other important body chemicals. DNA also includes information to control which genes are expressed and when, in all the cells of the body.

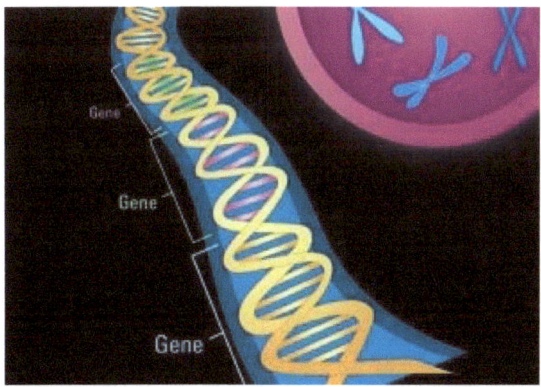

Fig2.

As we grow, we create new cells, each with a copy of our original set of DNA. Sometimes this copying process is imperfect, leading to a gene mutation that causes the gene to code for a slightly different protein. Some mutations are harmless, some can be helpful, and others give rise to disabilities or diseases.

Genes aren't the only determinants of how our bodies function. Throughout our lives, our genes can be affected by the environment. In medicine, the term environment includes not only our physical surroundings but also factors that can affect our bodies, such as sleep, diet, or stress. These factors may act alone or together in complex ways, to change the way a gene is expressed or the way messages are conducted in the body.

Epigenetics is the study of how environmental factors can affect how a given gene operates. But unlike gene mutations, epigenetic changes do not change the code for a gene. Rather, they effect when a gene turns on or off to produce a specific protein.

Scientists believe epigenetics play a major role in mental disorders and the effects of medications. Some, but not all mutations and epigenetic changes can be passed on to future generations.

Further understanding of genes and epigenetics may one day lead to genetic testing for people at risk for mental disorders. This could greatly help in early detection, more tailored treatments, and possibly prevention of such illnesses.

Everything we do relies on neurons communicating with one another. Electrical impulses and chemical signals carrying messages across different parts of the brain and between the brain and the rest of the nervous system. When a neuron is activated a small difference in electrical charge occurs. This unbalanced charge is called an action potential and is caused by the concentration of ions (atoms or molecules with unbalanced charges) across the cell membrane. The action potential travels very quickly along the axon, like when a line of dominoes falls.

When the action potential reaches the end of an axon, most neurons release a chemical message (a neurotransmitter) which crosses the synapse and binds to receptors on the receiving neuron's dendrites and starts the process over again. At the end of the line, a neurotransmitter may stimulate a different kind of cell (like a gland cell), or may trigger a new chain of messages.

Neurotransmitters send chemical messages between neurons. Mental illnesses, such as depression, can occur when this process does not work correctly. Communication between neurons can also be electrical, such as in areas of the brain that control movement. When electrical signals are abnormal, they can cause tremors or symptoms found in Parkinson's disease.

- **Serotonin**—helps control many functions, such as mood, appetite, and sleep. Research shows that people with depression often have lower than normal levels of serotonin. The types of medications most commonly prescribed to treat depression act by blocking the recycling, or reuptake, of serotonin by the sending neuron. As a result, more serotonin stays in the synapse for the receiving neuron to bind onto, leading to more normal mood functioning.

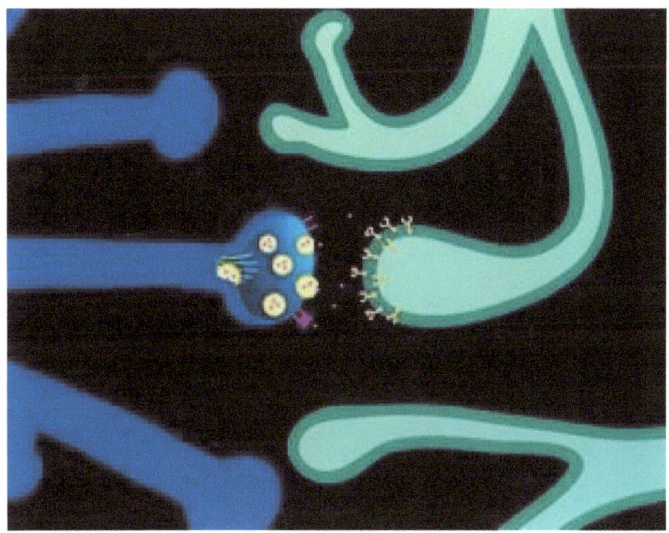

Fig3.

- **Dopamine**—mainly involved in controlling movement and aiding the flow of information to the front of the brain, which is linked to thought and emotion. It is also linked to reward systems in the brain. Problems in producing dopamine can result in Parkinson's disease, a disorder that affects a person's ability to move as they want to, resulting in stiffness, tremors or shaking, and other symptoms. Some studies suggest that having too little dopamine or problems using dopamine in the thinking and feeling regions of the brain may play a role in disorders like schizophrenia or attention deficit hyperactivity disorder (ADHD).

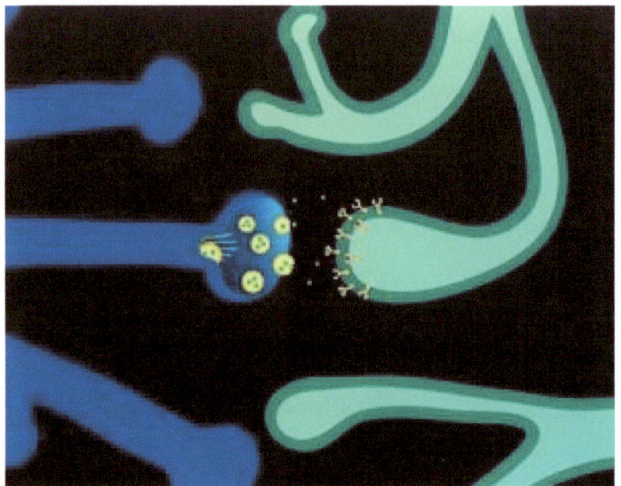

Fig 4.

- **Glutamate**—the most common neurotransmitter, glutamate has many roles throughout the brain and nervous system. Glutamate is an excitatory transmitter: when it is released it increases the chance that the neuron will fire. This enhances the electrical flow among brain cells required for normal function and plays an important role during early brain development. It may also assist in learning and memory. Problems in making or using glutamate have been linked to many mental disorders, including autism, obsessive compulsive disorder (OCD), schizophrenia, and depression.

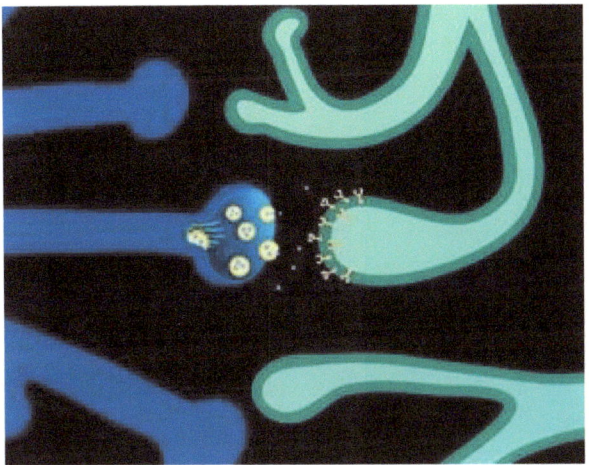

Fig 5.

Just as many neurons working together form a circuit, many circuits working together form specialized brain systems. We have many specialized brain systems that work across specific brain regions to help us talk, help us make sense of what we see, and help us to solve a problem. Some of the region's most commonly studied in mental health research are listed below.

- **Amygdala**—The brain's "fear hub," which activates our natural "fight-or-flight" response to confront or escape from a dangerous situation. The amygdala also appears to be involved in learning to fear an event, such as touching a hot stove, and learning not to fear, such as overcoming a fear of spiders. Studying how the amygdala helps create memories of fear and safety may help improve treatments for anxiety disorders like phobias or post-traumatic stress disorder (PTSD).
- **Prefrontal cortex (PFC)**—Seat of the brain's executive functions, such as judgment, decision making, and problem solving. Different parts of the PFC are involved in using short-term or "working" memory and in retrieving long-term memories. This area of the brain also helps to control the amygdala during stressful events. Some research shows that people who have PTSD or ADHD have reduced activity in their PFCs.

- **Anterior cingulate cortex (ACC)**— the ACC has many different roles, from controlling blood pressure and heart rate to responding when we sense a mistake, helping us feel motivated and stay focused on a task, and managing proper emotional reactions. Reduced ACC activity or damage to this brain area has been linked to disorders such as ADHD, schizophrenia, and depression.
- **Hippocampus**—Helps create and file new memories. When the hippocampus is damaged, a person can't create new memories, but can still remember past events and learned skills, and carry on a conversation, all which rely on different parts of the brain. The hippocampus may be involved in mood disorders through its control of a major mood circuit called the hypothalamic-pituitary-adrenal (HPA) axis.

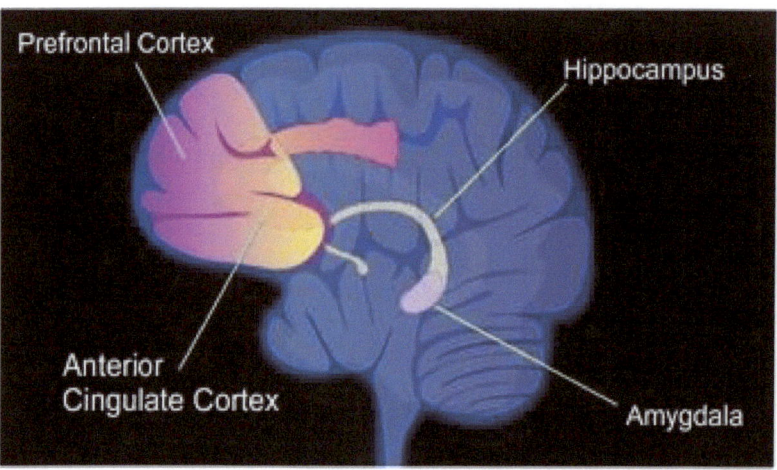

Fig 6.

Current Treatments for Bipolar II and GAD

Having GAD with Bipolar II can be a little difficult to treat because Antidepressants can make bipolar disorder worse. Even though antidepressants are a standard treatment for anxiety problems the recommendation is to treat the bipolar disorder first, then if anxiety symptoms remain, treat them.
The real meaning is If symptoms remain, "treat them" with a psychotherapy if at all possible rather than an antidepressant. There are excellent therapies with good results. If after the therapy has been tried, an antidepressant still must be considered, it should be added to mood stabilizers already.

When a diagnosis of GAD is made, the patient should be informed about the extent of overlap with bipolar disorder and an effort made to determine if the patient might have bipolar disorder. If after that the patient prefers to start with an antidepressant (versus psychotherapy, if available; or a mood stabilizer trial), we can't forget to look for hypomania or cycling of mood and energy in the first few months.
The trick is to make sure the treatment for the one doesn't make the other worse. That can be done.

The two main treatments for generalized anxiety disorder are psychotherapy and medications. You may benefit most from a combination of the two. It may take some trial and error to discover which treatments work best for you.

Talk therapy or psychological counseling, psychotherapy involves working with a therapist to reduce your anxiety symptoms. It can be an effective treatment for generalized anxiety disorder.

Cognitive behavioral therapy is one of the most effective forms of psychotherapy for generalized anxiety disorder. Generally a short-term treatment, cognitive behavioral therapy focuses on teaching you specific skills to gradually return to the activities you've avoided because of anxiety. Through this process, your symptoms improve as you build on your initial success.

Antidepressants, including medications in the selective serotonin reuptake inhibitor (SSRI) and serotonin norepinephrine reuptake inhibitor (SNRI) classes, are the first-line medication treatments. Examples of antidepressants used to treat anxiety disorders include escitalopram (Lexapro), duloxetine (Cymbalta), venlafaxine (Effexor XR) and paroxetine (Paxil, Pexeva).

Antidepressants selective reuptake inhibitors as SSRIs or SNRI classes works affecting our brain cells, or neurons communication. For SSRIs serotonin is released and for SNRI norepinephrine is release from the "sending" nerve cell, the leftover is normally reabsorbed by an uptake pump. By blocking the uptake pump, increases the amount of active serotonin & norepinephrine that can be delivered to the "receiving" nerve cell. This means that the neurons steep for a longer period of time in the serotonin & norepinephrine you already produce. There are other mechanisms as well. The drug blocks the sensor on the axon that tells the cell when enough serotonin has been produced. This causes the axon to release even more serotonin or norepinephrine. Finally, over a period of 2-3 weeks, the receiving cell becomes more sensitive to serotonin or norepinephrine, and this is the point at which the anti-depressant effect becomes experienced by the patient. It will take several more weeks, however, for the anti-obsessional effects to become completely realized.

It is possible to have too much serotonin or norepinephrine. Taking too much SSRI or SNRI medication, or other drugs that result in increased levels of serotonin in the body, can cause a problem called serotonin syndrome. The symptoms of this syndrome include changes in mental status (confusion, agitation, mania, anxiety, coma), cardiovascular function (irregular heartbeat, high or low blood pressure), gastrointestinal problems (nausea, diarrhea, abdominal pain), movement problems (muscle contractions or rigidity, restlessness, shaking, loss of coordination, shivering, seizures), and other serious problems.

Patients who abruptly stop certain SSRIs will develop some unpleasant discontinuation symptoms as the brain struggles to regain equilibrium. Symptoms may include headache, nausea, dizziness, insomnia and agitation, when allowed to run its course, this problem usually lasts from one to several weeks, and ranges from mild-moderate intensity in most patients, to extremely distressing in a small number. This is why SSRIs should always be slowly tapered off and never abruptly stopped.

Buspirone. An anti-anxiety medication called buspirone may be used on an ongoing basis. As with most antidepressants, it typically takes up to several weeks to become fully effective.

Benzodiazepines may be prescribe for one of these sedatives for relief of anxiety symptoms. Examples include alprazolam (Niravam, Xanax), chlordiazepoxide (Librium), diazepam (Valium) and lorazepam (Ativan). Benzodiazepines are generally used only for relieving acute anxiety on a short-term basis. Because they can be habit-forming, these medications aren't a good choice if you've had problems with alcohol or drug abuse.

Hypomania often masquerades as happiness and relentless optimism. When hypomania is not causing unhealthy behavior, it often may go unnoticed and therefore remain untreated. This is in contrast to full mania, which by definition causes problems in functioning and requires treatment with medications and possibly hospitalizations.

People with bipolar II disorder can benefit from preventive drugs that level out moods over the long term. These prevent the negative consequences of hypomania, and also help to prevent episodes of depression.

For Bipolar Mood Stabilizers like Lithium are used: This simple metal in pill form is highly effective at controlling mood swings (particularly highs) in bipolar disorder. Lithium has been used for more than 60 years to treat bipolar disorder. Lithium can take weeks to work fully, making it better for long-term treatment than for acute hypomanic episodes. Blood levels of lithium and other laboratory tests (such as kidney and thyroid functioning) must be monitored periodically to avoid side effects.

Carbamazepine (Tegretol): This antiseizure drug has been used to treat mania since the 1970s. Its possible value for treating bipolar depression, or preventing future highs and lows, is less well-established. Blood tests to monitor liver functioning and white blood cell counts also are periodically necessary.

Lamotrigine (Lamictal): This drug is approved by the FDA for the maintenance treatment of adults with bipolar disorder. It has been found to help delay bouts of mood episodes of depression, mania, hypomania (a milder form of mania), and mixed episodes in people being treated with standard therapy. It is especially helpful in preventing lows.

Valproate (Depakote): This antiseizure drug also works to level out moods. It has a more rapid onset of action than lithium, and it can also be used "off label" for prevention of highs and lows.

Some other antiseizure medications, such as gabapentin (Neurontin), oxcarbazapine (Trileptal), and topiramate (Topamax) are also sometimes prescribed as "experimental" (less-proven) treatments for mood symptoms or associated features in people with bipolar disorder.

Antipsychotics by definition, hypomanic episodes do not involve psychosis and do not interfere with functioning. Antipsychotic drugs, such as aripiprazole (Abilify), cariprazine (Vraylar), quetiapine (Seroquel), asenapine (Saphris), olanzapine (Zyprexa), risperidone (Risperdal), and ziprasidone (Geodon) and others, are nevertheless sometimes used in hypomania and some (notably, Seroquel) are used for depression in bipolar II disorder.

Benzodiazepines as in GAD are used including alprazolam (Xanax), diazepam (Valium), and lorazepam (Ativan) and is commonly referred to as minor tranquilizers. They are used for short-term control of acute symptoms associated with hypomania such as insomnia or agitation.

Other antipsycotic Seroquel and Seroquel XR is the only medication FDA-approved specifically for bipolar II depression.

Psychotherapy, such as cognitive-behavioral therapy, may also help.

Because bipolar II disorder typically involves recurrent episodes, continuous and ongoing treatment with medicines is often recommended for relapse prevention.

A critical view of Benzodiazepines.

The use of benzodiazepines for GAD or anything including recreational drug is a really hot topic and difficult to get into conclusions. Should be used or not for GAD?. Good question.

Reading in the Internet you found that there have been several highly publicized deaths from combining pain pills with benzodiazepines. The medications are commonly prescribed, and there are a number of misconceptions among laypeople about their proper use. The literature published in internet in most cases said that the non-medical community associates SSRI's like Prozac or Zoloft with antidepressants, and believes that the proper treatments for anxiety disorders are sedatives like Valium or Xanax (Benzos). Most web sites publish that benzos are sedatives useful in some situations, for example acute or short-term anxiety;   for chronic anxiety, the proper treatment consists of SSRIs or closely-related SNRIs.

Benzos have been target by medical sites as medications which are dangerous for addicts, and are intended for short-term use. Benzodiazepines CAUSE attention problems; in fact, Benzodiazepines treat anxiety by preventing the brain from attending, attaching and remembering. Anesthesiologists and dentists use the short-acting benzodiazepine midazolam during uncomfortable procedures to block memory.

All Benzos have appropriate uses, almost always for short-term conditions. When given long-term, they cause problems. Even if the medication is truly helpful, her relief will be short-lived due to tolerance. The human body quickly adjusts to benzodiazepines (and many other medications) so that a continued effect requires a higher and higher dose. Patients often escalate their dose at some point, no matter how many times they promise that they won't. Benzodiazepines turn manageable anxiety into an anxiety disorder. Patients get a calming effect from the medication, but as the medication wears off, the anxiety returns, including extra anxiety from a rebound effect.

Benzodiazepines impair driving and working with dangerous machinery. Benzos have been linked to fetal anomalies and early miscarriage. They destroy sleep in the long run through tolerance and through rebound effects. If the patient takes a benzodiazepine during the day, he or she will go to bed just as the sedation is wearing off. The alternative is to take the medication at bedtime, defeating the goal of finding relief for daytime anxiety. If the person takes benzodiazepines both day and night, tolerance increases even more quickly. Benzodiazepines and the risk of seizures (and worse) during withdrawal. Finally, Benzodiazepines may calm an anxious person, but they do not generally increase function.

In reality Benzos presents a unique set of clinical, ethical, and legal dilemmas in combination. Benzodiazepines are invaluable therapeutic agents which (in varying degrees) may produce physiological dependence; moreover, their use may complicate or be complicated by the abuse of other substances. In prescribing these controlled substances, more than with other medications, physicians may be perceived to be acting as agents of the state as well as of the patient, with the potential for ethical conflict that this dual role entails.

In some circumstances it may be unethical to prescribe benzodiazepines; in other circumstances it may be unethical to withhold them, even if prescribing involves risks for the clinician. Benzodiazepines suffer from guilt by association, in that the clinician who treats street-drug users will often see benzodiazepines used to self-medicate the consequences of that abuse. On the other hand, the clinician who treats a more heterogeneous population may see Valium (diazepam) misuse, but will not see true addiction, insofar as there is no dose escalation or compulsive use in spite of adverse consequences. As with insulin and digitalis, drugs needed for long-term therapeutic use may produce dependence, but that is not the same as addiction. The closest that benzodiazepine abuse comes to addiction is as part of a pattern of poly-drug abuse, sometimes with the rationalization that other chemical addictions require, in compensation, increasing dosages of benzodiazepines.

Long-term therapeutic use of benzodiazepines occurs primarily in three groups of patients. The largest group is those with chronic, serious medical illnesses (e.g., cardiovascular). It would be cruel to deny to these patients, often well advanced in age, the degree of relief offered by benzodiazepines. The second group is those with panic disorder. Whether benzodiazepines are more appropriate for such individuals than SSRIs or other antidepressants must be decided by weighing therapeutic versus side effects on a case-by-case basis. However, there is no evidence of benzodiazepine abuse in this population, and chronic use tends to result in gradual dose reduction over time. The third group consists of individuals with chronic psychiatric disorders or repeated instances of acute stress for example GAD as myself. It will be cruel to deny me Klonoping, or Xanax which are the only drugs in combination with Antipsychotic (Seroquel XR), Antidepressant as Paxil (SSRS) & Mizartapine that stop in those days the terrible anxiety stages when I get paralyzed. Here, too, except for those with personality disorders, much chronic benzodiazepine use and pharmacological dependence occur in the context of legitimate treatment.

Disagreements between clinicians concerned mainly with overuse of benzodiazepines and those who focus on underuse are based in part on different perspectives, patient populations, and values. Unfortunately, the salient dimensions of what should be a clinical controversy have all too often been obscured by the misuse of the term "addiction," which has created a false analogy between benzodiazepine dependence and addiction to substances of abuse.

 Ethical and legal dilemmas begin as clinical dilemmas, sometimes exacerbated by the constraints of managed health care. Special care needs to be taken, therefore, when evaluating and treating a variety of vulnerable populations, including the pregnant patient, institutionalized populations, such as geriatric residents of nursing homes and inmates in correctional settings, people who live alone or who have a history of abuse or a disordered family situation, patients being treated with methadone, and patients who are facing stresses such as examinations or testifying in court. Given that many alcohol and drug abusers also abuse benzodiazepines, a careful psychiatric examination, substance-abuse screening, and the recognition of biopsychosocial signs of abuse are imperative. All of the above is easier said than done, given the increasing time pressures and devaluation of time spent with patients on the part of many managed-care reimbursement schemes.

By getting to know the patient over a period of time, the physician can prescribe with a deeper understanding and greater confidence that the patient will work out any resulting problems within rather than outside the alliance. Managed health care, by putting a premium on short hospital stays, short-term therapies, and the fifteen-minute psychopharmacological or internist patient visit, often precludes long-term alliance building. Physicians feel compelled not only to prescribe benzodiazepines without adequate knowledge of the patient, but even to use these drugs as substitutes for listening to and talking with patients.

"Any drug likely to impair driving performance should be tried by the patient for a week without driving," and that, more pointedly, "Failure to inform patients of the risks of driving while on medication may lead to a claim of negligence against the prescribing.

Real Life Anxiety with Bipolar II

Medicine alone is not enough. Several good life changes must or should be made to improve a person having Bipolar II / Anxiety.
Having bipolar disorder comes in a variety of forms for different people, and it is much more than just having depression and mania or Hypomania.

I recommend to focus on helping yourself, and also others with same or similar conditions to stop negative substances. Also, without talking about religion been more spiritual is a plus. I think is a purpose of why we have mental disorders and living it is a Journal like other obstacles or challenges in life. Anything counts. Focus in small goals and things will get better. When you are in crisis look for help; believe me you need it. Don't make important decisions when you feel bad or High.

For me for example I got three divorces and two of them were bad decisions. Some of the arguments that ended in divorce were Bipolar and anxious. Once you get in some control of Bipolar and Anxiety is a good time to visualize. I'm 45 now and yes I have amazing kids, etc. I personally feel that the big purpose in my life is taking care of me now, my health, my children, keep family and great friends close, helping others, being a messenger to stop the Stigma of Mental Disorders, and find a good woman that love me with my Bag including Bipolar II and anxiety.

Medications are super important and always remember that missing pills because you feel better could end yourself from a normal happy human been to someone just capable to barely able to hold a spoon to the mouth. Trust me on this. I live it. Don't touch your medications at least a professional mandate.

We having Bipolar and in my case Anxiety also; need to be clear that the real world is not Mania or Hypomania. That when medicated those high intensity feelings is now in the past. We were sick, and they were valid feelings; but we could not live a stable life with more peace for us and love ones.

Being well medicated make us more responsibly, maintain a long-term relationship, and able to make informed and sound decisions.

Living or taking care of a person with Bipolar disorder will take a toll. Living well with bipolar disorder requires certain adjustments. Like recovering alcoholics who avoid drinking or diabetics who take insulin, if you have bipolar disorder, it's important to make healthy choices for yourself. Making these healthy choices will help you keep your symptoms under control, minimize mood episodes, and take control of your life.

Managing bipolar disorder starts with proper treatment, including medication and therapy. But there is so much more you can do to help yourself on a day-to-day basis. The daily decisions you make influence the course of your illness: whether your symptoms get better or worse; whether you stay well or experience a relapse; and how quickly you rebound from a mood episode.

- **Hope.** With good symptom management, it is possible to experience long periods of wellness. Believing that you can cope with your mood disorder is both accurate and essential to recovery.
- **Perspective.** Depression and manic-depression often follow cyclical patterns. Although you may go through some painful times and it may be difficult to believe things will get better, it is important not to give up hope.

- **Personal Responsibility.** It's up to you to take action to keep your moods stabilized. This includes asking for help from others when you need it, taking your medication as prescribed and keeping appointments with your health care providers.
- **Self-Advocacy.** Become an effective advocate for yourself so you can get the services and treatment you need, and make the life you want for yourself.
- **Education.** Learn all you can about your illness. This allows you to make informed decisions about all aspects of your life and treatment.
- **Support.** Working toward wellness is up to you. However, support from others is essential to maintaining your stability and enhancing the quality of your life.

Be a full and active participant in your own treatment. Learn everything you can about bipolar disorder. Become an expert on the illness. Study up on the symptoms, so you can recognize them in yourself, and research all your available treatment options. The more informed you are, the better prepared you'll be to deal with symptoms and make good choices for yourself.

Using what you've learned about bipolar disorder, collaborate with your doctor or therapist in the treatment planning process. Don't be afraid to voice your opinions or questions. The most beneficial relationships between patient and healthcare provider work as a partnership. You may find it helpful to draw up a treatment contract outlining the goals you and your provider have agreed upon.

Other tips for successful bipolar disorder treatment:

- **Be patient.** Don't expect an immediate and total cure. Have patience with the treatment process. It can take time to find the right program that works for you.
- **Communicate with your treatment provider.** Your treatment program will change over time, so keep in close contact with your doctor or therapist. Talk to your provider if your condition or needs change and be honest about your symptoms and any medication side effects.
- **Take your medication as instructed.** If you're taking medication, follow all instructions and take it faithfully. Don't skip or change your dose without first talking with your doctor.
- **Get therapy.** While medication may be able to manage some of the symptoms of bipolar disorder, therapy teaches you skills you can use in all areas of your life. Therapy can help you learn how to deal with your disorder, cope with problems, regulate your mood, change the way you think, and improve your relationships.

In order to stay well, it's important to be closely attuned to the way you feel. By the time obvious symptoms of mania or depression appear, it is often too late to intercept the mood swing, so keep a close watch for subtle changes in your mood, sleeping patterns, energy level, and thoughts. If you catch the problem early and act swiftly, you may be able to prevent a minor mood change from turning into a full-blown episode of mania or depression.

Know your triggers and early warning signs—and watch for them

It's important to recognize the warning signs of an oncoming manic or depressive episode. Make a list of early symptoms that preceded your previous mood episodes. Also try to identify the triggers, or outside influences, that have led to mania or depression in the past. Common triggers include:

- stress
- financial difficulties
- arguments with your loved ones
- problems at school or work
- seasonal changes
- lack of sleep

Common red flags for bipolar disorder relapse

Warning signs of depression

- I quit cooking meals.
- I no longer want to be around people.
- I crave chocolate.
- I start having headaches.
- I don't care about anybody else.
- People bother me.
- I start needing more sleep, including naps during the day.

Warning signs of mania or hypomania

- I find myself reading five books at once.
- I can't concentrate.
- I find myself talking faster than usual.
- I feel irritable.
- I'm hungry all the time.
- Friends tell me that I'm crabby.
- I need to move around because I have more energy than usual.

Knowing your early warning signs and triggers won't do you much good if you aren't keeping close tabs on how you're feeling. By checking in with yourself through regular mood monitoring, you can be sure that red flags don't get lost in the shuffle of your busy, daily life.

Keeping a mood chart is one way to monitor your symptoms and moods. A mood chart is a daily log of your emotional state and other symptoms you're having. It can also include information such as how many hours of sleep you're getting, your weight, medications you're taking, and any alcohol or drug use. You can use your mood chart to spot patterns and indicators of trouble ahead.

If you spot any warning signs of mania or depression, it's important to act swiftly. In such times, it's helpful to have a wellness toolbox to draw from. A wellness toolbox consists of coping skills and activities you can do to maintain a stable mood or to get better when you're feeling "off."

The coping techniques that work best will be unique to your situation, symptoms, and preferences. It takes experimentation and time to find a winning strategy. However, many people with bipolar disorder have found the following tools to be helpful in reducing symptoms and maintaining wellness:

- talk to a supportive person
- get a full eight hours of sleep
- cut back on your activities
- attend a support group
- call your doctor or therapist
- do something fun or creative
- take time for yourself to relax and unwind
- write in your journal
- exercise
- ask for extra help from loved ones
- cut back on sugar, alcohol, and caffeine
- increase your exposure to light
- increase or decrease the stimulation in your environment

Create an emergency action plan

Despite your best efforts, there may be times when you experience a relapse into full-blown mania or severe depression. In crisis situations where your safety is at stake, your loved ones or doctor may have to take charge of your care. Such times can leave you feeling helpless and out of control, but having a crisis plan in place allows you to maintain some degree of responsibility for your own treatment.

A plan of action typically includes:

- A list of emergency contacts (your doctor, therapist, close family members)
- A list of all medications you are taking, including dosage information
- Information about any other health problems you have
- Symptoms that indicate you need others to take responsibility for your care

- Treatment preferences (who you want to care for you; what treatments and medications do and do not work, who is authorized to make decisions on your behalf)

Reaching out and building relationships

1. Talk to one person about your feelings.
2. Help someone else by volunteering.
3. Have lunch or coffee with a friend.
4. Ask a loved one to check in with you regularly.
5. Accompany someone to the movies, a concert, or a small get-together.
6. Call or email an old friend.
7. Go for a walk with a workout buddy.
8. Schedule a weekly dinner date
9. Meet new people by taking a class or joining a club.
10. Confide in a counselor, therapist, or clergy member.

Having a strong support system is vital to staying happy and healthy. Often, simply having someone to talk to face to face can be an enormous help in relieving bipolar depression and boosting your outlook and motivation. The people you turn to don't have to be able to "fix" you; they just have to be good listeners.

- **Turn to friends and family** – Support for bipolar disorder starts close to home. It's important to have people you can count on to help you through rough times. Isolation and loneliness can cause depression, so regular contact with supportive friends and family members is therapeutic in itself. Reaching out to others is not a sign of weakness and it won't make you a burden. Your loved ones care about you and want to help.
- **Join a bipolar disorder support group** – Spending time with people who know what you're going through and can honestly say they've "been there" can be very therapeutic. You can also benefit from the shared experiences and advice of the group members. To find a support group in your area, see Resources section below.
- **Build new relationships** – Isolation and loneliness make bipolar disorder worse. If you don't have a support network you can count on, take steps to **develop new relationships**. Try taking a class, joining a church or a civic group, volunteering, or attending events in your community.

Your lifestyle choices, including your sleeping, eating, and exercise patterns, have a significant impact on your moods. There are many things you can do in your daily life to get your symptoms under control and to keep depression and mania at bay.

- **Build structure into your life.** Developing and sticking to a daily schedule can help stabilize the mood swings of bipolar disorder. Include set times for sleeping, eating, socializing, exercising, working, and relaxing. Try to maintain a regular pattern of activity, even through emotional ups and downs.
- **Exercise regularly. Exercise has a beneficial impact on mood** and may reduce the number of bipolar episodes you experience. Aerobic exercise is especially effective at treating depression. Try to incorporate at least 30 minutes of activity five times a week into your routine. Walking is a good choice for people of all fitness levels.
- **Keep a strict sleep schedule.** Getting too little sleep can trigger mania, so it's important to get plenty of rest. For some people, losing even a few hours can cause problems. However, too much sleep can also worsen your mood. The best advice is to **maintain a consistent sleep schedule**.

Healthy sleep habits for managing bipolar disorder

- Go to bed and wake up at the same time each day.
- Avoid or minimize napping, especially if it interferes with your sleep at night.
- Avoid exercising or doing other stimulating activities late in the day.
- No caffeine after lunch or alcohol at night. Both interfere with sleep.

Stress can trigger episodes of mania and depression in people with bipolar disorder, so keeping it under control is extremely important. Know your limits, both at home and at work or school. Don't take on more than you can handle and take time to yourself if you're feeling overwhelmed.

- **Learn how to relax. Relaxation techniques** such as deep breathing, meditation, yoga, and guided imagery can be very effective at reducing stress and keeping you on an even keel. A daily relaxation practice of 30 minutes or more can improve your mood and keep depression at bay.
- **Make leisure time a priority.** Do things for no other reason than that it feels good to do them. Go to a funny movie, take a walk on the beach, listen to music, read a good book, or talk to a friend. Doing things just because they are fun is no indulgence. Play is an emotional and mental health necessity.
- **Appeal to your senses. Stay calm and energized by appealing to your senses**: sight, sound, touch, smell, and taste. Listen to music that lifts your mood, place flowers where you will see and smell them, massage your hands and feet, or sip a warm drink.

rom the food you eat to the vitamins and drugs you take, the substances you put in your body have an impact on the symptoms of bipolar disorder—both for better or worse.

- **Eat a healthy diet.** There is an undeniable link between food and mood. For optimal mood, eat plenty of fresh fruits, vegetables, and whole grains and limit your fat and sugar intake. Space your meals out through the day, so your blood sugar never dips too low. High-carbohydrate diets can cause mood crashes, so they should also be avoided. Other mood-damaging foods include chocolate, caffeine, and processed foods.
- **Get your omega-3s.** Omega-3 fatty acids may decrease mood swings in bipolar disorder. Omega-3 is available as a nutritional supplement. You can also increase your intake of omega-3 by eating cold-water fish such as salmon, halibut, and sardines, soybeans, flaxseeds, canola oil, pumpkin seeds, and walnuts.
- **Avoid alcohol and drugs.** Drugs such as cocaine, ecstasy, and amphetamines can trigger mania, while alcohol and tranquilizers can trigger depression. Even moderate social drinking can upset your emotional balance. Substance use also interferes with sleep and may cause dangerous interactions with your medications. Attempts to self-medicate or numb your symptoms with drugs and alcohol only create more problems.
- **Be cautious when taking any medication.** Certain prescription and over-the-counter medications can be problematic for people with bipolar disorder. Be especially careful with antidepressant drugs, which can trigger mania. Other drugs that can cause mania include over-the-counter cold medicine, appetite suppressants, caffeine, corticosteroids, and thyroid medication.

Religion and Bipolar II & Anxiety.

This is a difficult topic to bring Religion in Mental Health; but I found a very good when I turned more to God. But Religion is not the right word ; I rather call Spiritual.

I gain strength against my anxiety and depression when I got more close to God. Great spirituality teaches that belief and strength are a great way to support your own mental health, and that it's our duty to take care of our emotions. Jesus teaches acceptance, both of the world and of oneself. Acceptance starts by understanding your anxiety further and really recognizing causes and solutions for your anxiety symptoms.

"For I know the plans I have for you, says the Lord. They are plans for good and not for disaster, to give you a future and a hope." Jeremiah 29:11-12

One of the reasons that people find get closer to God is that helps them overcome anxiety is because at the core of anxiety is fear. Fear over the unknown and the belief that specific things in your life are important.

Christianity teaches values that promote less anxiety, specifically because the beliefs in Christianity runs directly counter to the issues that cause anxiety. **Fear of the Unknown.** The bible teaches that fear of the unknown shows a lack of faith in God. Everything is supposed to be the result of God's plan. If you're allowing yourself to be overcome by anxiety and fear, then you're showing that you don't have trust in God. The more trust you have, the more confident you are in change and what happens in the future.

- **Fear of Death** death isn't something to fear at all. In fact, a life lived in God's path is designed to help you get to heaven, which is the ultimate goal of Christianity. This is seen in many Christians that adopt the religion after experiencing profound stress. Jesus gives their life purpose, which helps them overcome this belief that passing is something they need to fear.

- **Personal Fears** Many people also have personal fears that affect them. For example, someone may fear embarrassment, or they may fear spiders, or they may fear socializing. All of these personal fears go against the belief in God, which is that your fears are selfish, when God has a plan for you. Personal fears can be hard to control, but a strong belief system can help people overcome that anxiety.

The core of believing in God is about trust over every uncertainty and fear in life and so this belief can be used to allow people to stop anxiety. If you believe in Christianity but still have anxiety, you may be asking what more you can do. That indicates that your relationship isn't as strong as you would like it to be. Consider the following tips to help use your belief to overcome anxiety:

- **Do More Than Pray for Relief praying** for relief of anxiety isn't truly living with God's plan. Belief is what helps you overcome anxiety, and strength of that trust is what allows you to feel less fear. Praying that God simply relieves your anxiety may actually make it worse, because God does believe in personal effort, and anxiety isn't something He is going to simply wash away.
- **Attend Church More** Church represents a constant reminder of your relationship with God. It's not just about making sure that you do what you need to do to get into Heaven and show God you love Him. It's also about making sure that you are reminded of your belief as often as possible, so that you are able to keep that relationship strong with each passing day.

- **Take Care of Your Body** _"Do you not know that your body is a temple of the Holy Spirit, who is in you, whom you have received from God? You are not your own - you were bought at a price. Therefore honor God with your body." 1 Corinthians 6:19-20. _Exercising an taking care of your body is actually ordered by God, and exercise is something that is known to cure anxiety. It is not a coincidence that God requires it.
- **Volunteer** Living for someone other than yourself is also a part of showing glory to God. Volunteering is a constant reminder of the values of humanity, which will bring you closer to your beliefs and build the Christian relationship inside of you. Find something you're passionate about and volunteer to it and see a real different in the way you find happiness in the world.
- **Focus on Your Beliefs** Finally, learn to get more in touch with the beliefs that you already have. The truth is that your beliefs can always be nurtured. Write down the beliefs that are important for showing faith in your Christianity, and continue to work towards them often so that you can continue to build on what you need to in order to rid yourself of anxiety.

The Christian relationship is a powerful one, and something that you can nurture in such a way that your anxiety is more likely to be countered as a result. Learn to address the beliefs that Christianity harbors and you may find that your anxiety is reduced as a result.

Also, don't forget to take advantage of what's available on this earth. Remember that God blessed the world with psychologists, medicines, research - these are not something that need to be looked at as an enemy to belief. Rather, they're something that God has offered as a way to improve upon one's life. You're not insulting God by looking to others for help. You're showing God that you're thankful for the help that He's made available to the world.

Matthew 6:25-34

25 "Therefore I tell you, do not worry about your life, what you will eat or drink; or about your body, what you will wear. Is not life more than food, and the body more than clothes? 26 Look at the birds of the air; they do not sow or reap or store away in barns, and yet your heavenly Father feeds them. Are you not much more valuable than they? 27 Can any one of you by worrying add a single hour to your life? 28 "And why do you worry about clothes? See how the flowers of the field grow. They do not labor or spin. 29 Yet I tell you that not even Solomon in all his splendor was dressed like one of these. 30 If that is how God clothes the grass of the field, which is here today and tomorrow is thrown into the fire, will he not much more clothe you—you of little faith? 31 So do not

worry, saying, 'What shall we eat?' or 'What shall we drink?' or 'What shall we wear?' 32 For the pagans run after all these things, and your heavenly Father knows that you need them. 33 But seek first his kingdom and his righteousness, and all these things will be given to you as well. 34 Therefore do not worry about tomorrow, for tomorrow will worry about itself. Each day has enough trouble of its own.

Proverbs 3:5-6

5Trust in the LORD with all your heart and lean not on your own understanding; 6 in all your ways submit to him, and he will make your paths straight.

Philippians 4:6-7

Do not be anxious about anything, but in every situation, by prayer and petition, with thanksgiving, present your requests to God. 7 And the peace of God, which transcends all understanding, will guard your hearts and your minds in Christ Jesus.

Luke 12:24-34

Consider the ravens: They do not sow or reap, they have no storeroom or barn; yet God feeds them. And how much more valuable you are than birds! 25 Who of you by worrying can add a single hour to your life? 26 Since you cannot do this very little thing, why do you worry about the rest? 27 "Consider how the wild flowers grow. They do not labor or spin. Yet I tell you, not even Solomon in all his splendor was dressed like one of these. 28 If that is how God clothes the grass of the field, which is here today, and tomorrow is thrown into the fire, how much more will he clothe you—you of little faith! 29 And do not set your heart on what you will eat or drink; do not worry about it. 30 For the pagan world runs after all such things, and your Father knows that you need them. 31 But seek his kingdom, and these things will be given to you as well. 32 "Do not be afraid, little flock, for your Father has been pleased to give you the kingdom. 33 Sell your possessions and give to the poor. Provide purses for yourselves that will not wear out, a treasure in heaven that will never fail, where no thief comes near and no moth destroys. 34 For where your treasure is, there your heart will be also.

Matthew 11:28-30

"Come to me, all you who are weary and burdened, and I will give you rest. 29 Take my yoke upon you and learn from me, for I am gentle and humble in heart, and you will find rest for your souls. 30 For my yoke is easy and my burden is light."

John 14:27

Peace I leave with you; my peace I give you. I do not give to you as the world gives. Do not let your hearts be troubled and do not be afraid.

Colossians 3:15

Let the peace of Christ rule in your hearts, since as members of one body you were called to peace. And be thankful.

Thessalonians 3:16

Now may the Lord of peace himself give you peace at all times and in every way. The Lord be with all of you.

Psalm 55:22

Cast your cares on the LORD and he will sustain you; he will never let the righteous be shaken.

Proverbs 12:25

Anxiety weighs down the heart, but a kind word cheers it up.

Peter 5:6-8

Humble yourselves, therefore, under God's mighty hand, that he may lift you up in due time. 7 Cast all your anxiety on him because he cares for you. 8 Be alert and of sober mind. Your enemy the devil prowls around like a roaring lion looking for someone to devour.

Psalm 23:4

Even though I walk through the darkest valley, I will fear no evil, for you are with me; your rod and your staff, they comfort me.

Hebrews 13:5-6

Keep your lives free from the love of money and be content with what you have, because God has said, "Never will I leave you; never will I forsake you." 6 So we say with confidence, "The Lord is my helper; I will not be afraid. What can mere mortals do to me?"

Psalm 56:3

When I am afraid, I put my trust in you.

The Future in Treatments for Bipolar II and Anxiety.

I will present this chapter as a collection of new technologies, studies, medicines and papers that can explain where the future is going with treatments. At the time you read this book they will probably better studies, but seems we are moving fast and strong. I hope USA, Europe and other countries push good finance for more research.

Technology#1

TMS or Transcranial magnetic stimulation therapy is a computerized electromechanical instrument that produces and delivers brief duration, rapidly alternating (pulsed) magnetic fields to induce electrical currents in localized regions of the cerebral cortex.
Is indicated for the treatment of Major Depressive Disorder in adult patients who have failed to receive satisfactory improvement from prior antidepressant medication in the current episode.

TMS is available upon the prescription of a licensed physician. It can be used in both inpatient and outpatient settings including physicians' offices, clinics, and hospitals.

TMS Therapy System produces a time varying magnetic field, its intended effect derives fundamentally from Faraday's Law, which asserts that a time-varying magnetic field produces an electrical current in an adjacent conductive substance. During TMS, the conductive substance of interest is the brain.

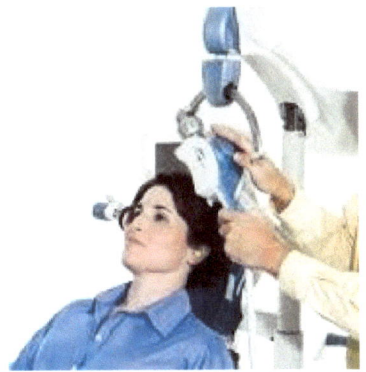

Fig.7

Technology#2

Deep Brain Stimulation or DBS.

Fifteen percent of Americans have clinical depression during some portion of their lives. A third of those have major depression: suicidal thoughts, a sense of disconnection from the world. For a few of those, the entire arsenal of traditional treatments — therapy, medications, even electroconvulsive therapy — doesn't work. These are the patients DBS can help.

The doctors implanted very thin wires with tiny electrodes in two small lobes deep at the brain. Precisely the placed the electrodes were based on extensive brain maps, both of activity in different regions of the brains of depressed patients and of the neural cables that connect these regions, allowing communication between them.

The electrodes' job is to deliver a small amount of electrical current to the specific region of the brain. This region, Area 25, serves as a kind of junction box, so adjusting activity here is like tuning the entire depression circuitry. The electrodes are connected to an implantable pulse generator (IPG), a pacemaker-like device placed under Stowe's collarbone. The IPG keeps a steady stream of low voltage flowing into the patient's brain.

As the electrodes are tested in the OR, patients often report an emotional weight being lifted instantaneously—one way the team knows the electrode is in the right place.

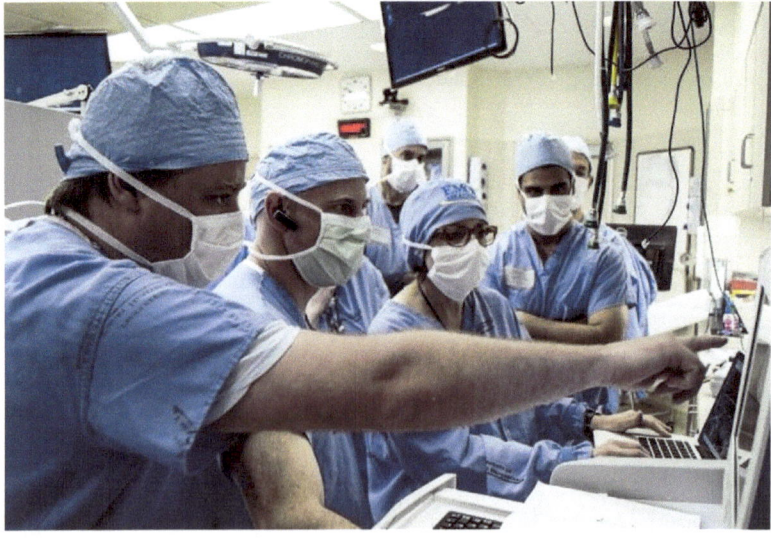

Fig. 8

Technology#3

Ablative procedure (cingulotomy)

Cingulotomy is brain surgery considered a last treatment resort for people with obsessive-compulsive disorder (OCD) major depression and sometimes chronic pain who haven't found relief from other forms of therapy. It's been suggested as a treatment for bipolar disorder, but it hasn't been well studied for that condition, and so is not recommended.

This surgery targets the region of the brain called the cingulate gyrus, which is a small area in the brain connecting the limbic system.

The limbic system is involved with many emotions. The surgery also targets the frontal lobes, whose functions include reasoning, impulse control and judgment.

Surgical procedures in psychiatry are controversial, and most doctors will not perform bilateral cingulotomy unless all other avenues of treatment for the patient's condition already have been tried. In some cases, neurosurgeons will seek consent for the surgery from both the patient and a close family member.

Rationale for Bilateral Cingulotomy

The brain's cingulate gyrus helps to regulate emotions and pain, including emotional responses to pain. It's also thought to regulate aggressive behavior. This region of the brain directly controls a person's response to bad experiences, and in turn, it helps the person avoid repeated bad experiences. This is an important part of learning and memory.

There's evidence that the limbic system plays a major role in obsessive-compulsive disorder and in other psychiatric conditions.

Therefore, psychiatrists and neurosurgeons believe that certain forms of brain surgery might help these conditions.

To perform a bilateral cingulotomy, an electrode or gamma knife (which focuses beams of radiation) is guided to the target area of the brain by means of a process known as stereotactic magnetic resonance imaging.

A small lesion is created there — about a 1/2 inch cut or burn. The idea is that this lesion will disrupt the circuits in the brain that lead to OCD-type behaviors or todepression.

Surgery Results

Bilateral cingulotomy appears to help some patients, but it's not a cure-all for these difficult-to-treat psychiatric conditions.

In one study, conducted by Harvard Medical School researchers, 44 patients with obsessive-compulsive disorder underwent the surgical procedure over the course of more than two decades. Those 44 people had not responded to medication or to behavioral treatments for their condition.

The researchers found that 32% to 45% of those treated with bilateral cingulotomy responded at least partially to the treatment.

In another small trial, this one conducted in China, researchers treated seven patients with obsessive-compulsive disorder with bilateral cingulotomy and bilateral capsulotomy, which is another form of brain surgery to treat OCD. In this study, five out of seven patients responded well to the surgery.

Possible Complications

Bilateral cingulotomy doesn't carry with it very many side effects. Some patients experience nausea and vomiting in the days following the surgery, and they may also experience headaches. The surgery may also trigger seizures in some people, although it's possible that those experiencing seizures following the surgery may have had a history of seizures before the surgery as well.

Following the surgery, some people complained of apathy, while others complained of memory lapses. However, these weren't common side effects of the procedure.

Unfortunately, bilateral cingulotomy doesn't eliminate the need for treatment of the mental condition — most people require ongoing treatment following the surgery, and some surgical teams require patients to remain in treatment. However, it does offer one option for people who haven't responded to other forms of treatment.

It's been suggested as a treatment for bipolar disorder, but it hasn't been well studied for that condition, and so is not recommended.

Study #1 In a Study in 2009 on Stanford University Medical Center (Scrambled connections between the part of the brain that processes fear and emotion and other brain regions could be the hallmark of a common anxiety disorder, according to a new study. The findings could help researchers identify biological differences between types of anxiety disorders as well as such disorders as depression.)

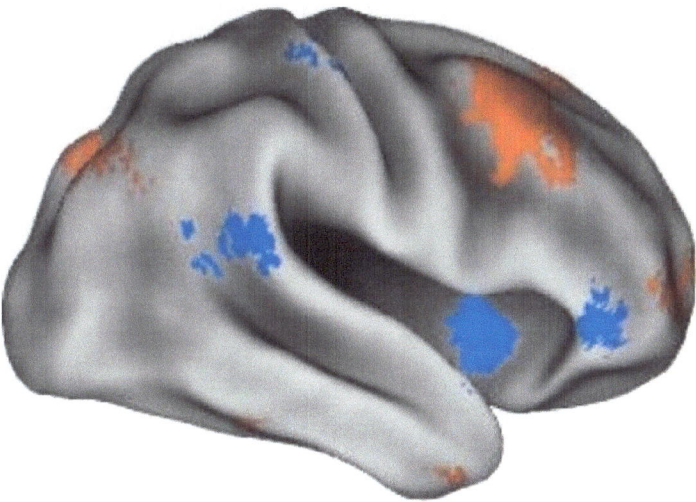

Fig.9

This image shows, in red, brain regions with stronger connections to the amygdala in patients with GAD, while the blue areas indicate weaker connectivity. The red corresponds to areas important for attention and may reflect the habitual use of cognitive strategies like worry and distraction in the anxiety patients.
Credit: Image courtesy of Stanford University Medical Center

This was an amazing study and even with the results we can't conclude how GAD really fully works; we can said for sure that there are differences in the communication / Chemistry of a GAD brain comparing with a called normal brain. It is important to recall that Researchers can't say for sure whether the connectivity abnormalities came first or whether excessive worrying shaped the brain by reinforcing particular neural pathways. Still, the patterns uncovered by neurological scans could one day help psychiatrists diagnose and treat the disease.

Another view and also interesting in my opinion to understand even deeply GAD is the component in neurons connectivity that causes the Chemistry imbalance. GAD patients does not have enough of the neurotransmitter called GABA (**gamma-Aminobutyric acid** "**γ-Aminobutyric acid** "). This is the boss inhibitory neurotransmitter in the human central nervous system. It plays the principal role in reducing neuronal excitability throughout the nervous system. In humans, GABA is also directly responsible for the regulation of muscle tone

GABA acts at inhibitory synapses in the brain by binding to specific transmembrane receptors in the plasma membrane of both pre- and postsynaptic neuronal processes. This binding causes the opening of ion channels to allow the flow of either negatively charged chloride ions into the cell or positively charged potassium ions out of the cell. This action results in a negative change in the transmembrane potential, usually causing hyperpolarization. Two general classes of GABA receptor are known: GABA$_A$ in which the receptor is part of a ligand-gated ion channel complex, and GABA$_B$ metabotropic receptors, which are G protein-coupled receptors that open or close ion channels via intermediaries (G proteins).

Neurons that produce GABA as their output are called GABAergic neurons, and have chiefly inhibitory action at receptors. Medium Spiny Cells are a typical example of inhibitory CNS GABAergic cells.

GABA$_A$ receptors are ligand-activated chloride channels; when activated by GABA, they allow the flow of chloride ions across the membrane of the cell. Whether this chloride flow is excitatory/depolarizing (makes the voltage across the cell's membrane less negative), shunting (has no effect on the cell's membrane potential) or inhibitory/hyperpolarizing (makes the cell's membrane more negative) depends on the direction of the flow of chloride. When net chloride flows out of the cell, GABA is excitatory or depolarizing; when chloride flows into the cell, GABA is inhibitory or hyperpolarizing. When the net flow of chloride is close to zero, the action of GABA is shunting. Shunting inhibition has no direct effect on the membrane potential of the cell; however, it reduces the effect of any coincident synaptic input by reducing the electrical resistance of the cell's membrane. A developmental switch in the molecular machinery controlling concentration of chloride inside the cell changes the functional role of GABA between neonatal and adult stages. As the brain develops into adulthood GABA's role changes from excitatory to inhibitory.

While GABA is an inhibitory transmitter in the mature brain, its actions are primarily excitatory in the developing brain. The gradient of chloride is reversed in immature neurons, and its reversal potential is higher than the resting membrane potential of the cell; activation of a GABA-A receptor thus leads to efflux of Cl^- ions from the cell, i.e. a depolarizing current. The differential gradient of chloride in immature neurons is primarily due to the higher concentration of NKCC1 co-transporters relative to KCC2 co-transporters in immature cells. GABA itself is partially responsible for orchestrating the maturation of ion pumps. GABA-ergic interneurons mature faster in the hippocampus and the GABA signaling machinery appears earlier than glutamatergic transmission. Thus, GABA is the major excitatory neurotransmitter in many regions of the brain before the maturation of glutamatergic synapses.

"This theory has been questioned based on results showing that in brain slices of immature mice incubated in artificial cerebrospinal fluid (ACSF) ".; but so far is been accepted and no paper as far as I know can probe it wrong.

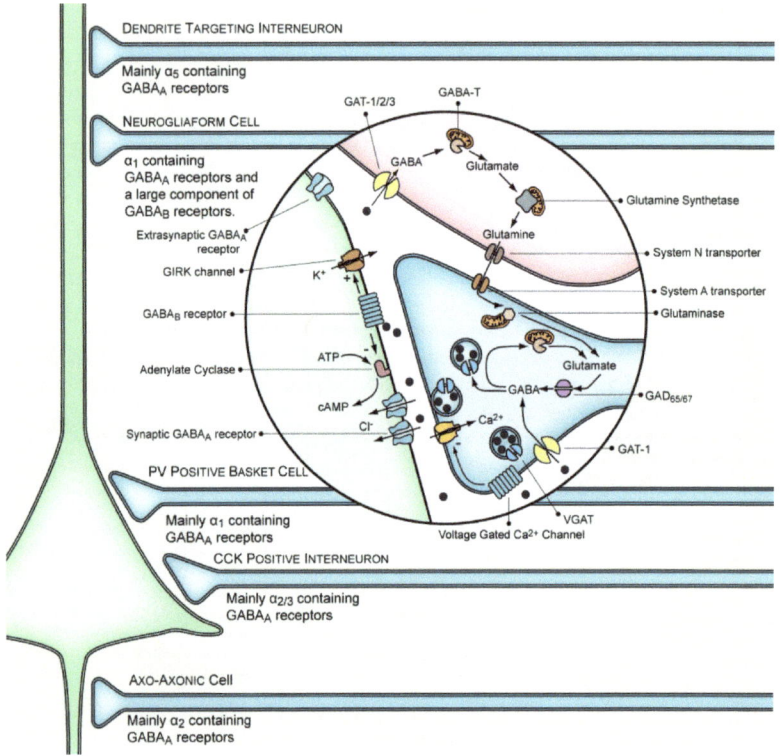

Fig. 10

Gamma-aminobutyric acid was first synthesized in 1883, and was first known only as a plant and microbe metabolic product. In 1950, however, GABA was discovered to be an integral part of the mammalian central nervous system.

External GABA does not penetrate the blood–brain barrier; it is synthesized in the brain. This is why supplements that are GABA does not work. It is synthesized from glutamate using the enzyme L-glutamic acid decarboxylase (GAD) and pyridoxal phosphate (which is the active form of vitamin B6) as a cofactor. This process converts glutamate, the principal excitatory neurotransmitter, into the principal inhibitory neurotransmitter (GABA). GABA is converted back to glutamate by a metabolic pathway called the GABA shunt.

Drugs that act as allosteric modulators of GABA receptors (known as GABA analogues or *GABAergic* drugs) or increase the available amount of GABA typically have relaxing, anti-anxiety, and anti-convulsive effects.

Study #2

Bipolar disorder, which affects nearly eight million Americans, takes a toll not only on patients, but also on their families and communities. In the new study, the researchers focused on a gene known as PDE10A, one of the many genes that has been linked to bipolar disorder, and the proteins this gene produces.

https://www.sciencedaily.com/releases/2016/03/160309125732.htm

Study #3

Older bipolar patients often have decreased activity in the hormone system responsible for the secretion of the stress hormone cortisol. Low levels of cortisol in bipolar patients were also associated with depression, low quality of life, obesity, dyslipidaemia and metabolic syndrome. These discoveries could provide important clues as to how treatment strategies for depression and bipolar disorder can be improved, according to a dissertation.

https://www.sciencedaily.com/releases/2016/01/160119074257.htm

Study #4

Acute stress can increase the presence of a key DNA modification called 5hmC throughout a portion of the brain called the hippocampus, vital in memory and learning, according to a study published in November 2015 in the journal *Neurobiology of Disease*. These modifications, observed in mice, may alter the activity of a variety of neurons and nerve signaling proteins in response to stress, and could be related to stress' effects on the brain in anxiety and traumatic stress disorders.

https://bbrfoundation.org/brain-matters-discoveries/researchers-track-gene-alterations-in-brain-area-perturbed-by-stress

Study #5

In animal research reported in the November 12 issue of the journal *Nature*, scientists have identified a specific region of the brain that helps regulate behaviors and physiological changes associated with anxiety. Cells in this area, known as the basomedial amygdala, differentiate between safe and potentially threatening environments, and work together to suppress anxiety when conditions seem safe.

Better understanding of how the brain regulates fear and anxiety is likely to help researchers develop more effective treatments for anxiety disorders.

https://bbrfoundation.org/brain-matters-discoveries/researchers-trace-anxiety-control-to-specific-brain-region

Study #6

By disrupting a single gene, scientists have created mice that excel at tasks involving memory and problem solving and exhibit less anxiety than normal mice. The research suggests that drugs targeting the protein encoded by the gene called phosphodiesterase-4B (PDE4B), might be useful in treating anxiety disorders or improving cognition (thinking) in people with dementia.

Steven J. Clapcote, Ph.D., a 2007 NARSAD Young Investigator, was the senior scientist on the international team, which included 2006 Distinguished Investigator John C. Roder, Ph.D.; 2007 Young Investigator John Georgiou, Ph.D.; and 2003 Young Investigator and 2006 Independent Investigator Fang Liu, M.D., Ph.D. Their study appeared August 14th in the journal *Neuropsychopharmacology*.

https://bbrfoundation.org/brain-matters-discoveries/anxiety-diminishes-and-memory-improves-when-single-gene-is-mutated-in-mice

Study #7

esearchers have found that by specifically targeting a central signaling pathway in the brain, they can improve the innate behavioral response to stress in mice. Stress-induced behaviors in rodents reflect many of the symptoms that affect people suffering from major depression and other clinical conditions associated with stress. The findings, published July 20th online in the journal*Nature Neuroscience*, suggest a new strategy for treating depression and other stress-associated disorders.

The study was led by James A. Bibb, Ph.D., at The University of Texas Southwestern Medical Center, who received NARSAD Young Investigator grants in 2000 and 2003, and lead authorFlorian Plattner, Ph.D. The scientific team also included Paul Greengard, Ph.D., a member of BBRF's Scientific Council and a 1992, 2002, and 2008 Distinguished Investigator; Eric J. Nestler, M.D., Ph.D., a Scientific Council Member and a 1996 Distinguished Investigator; 2006 Young Investigator Kanehiro Hayashi, Ph.D.; 2007 Young Investigator Eunice Y. Yuen, Ph.D.; 1999 and 2004 Young Investigator Zhen Yan, Ph.D.; and 1999 Independent Investigator and 2006 Distinguished Investigator Angus C. Nairn, Ph.D.

https://bbrfoundation.org/brain-matters-discoveries/blocking-key-signaling-pathway-in-brain-improves-stress-response-in-mice

Study #8

Although the symptoms of generalized social anxiety disorder are sometimes alleviated by antidepressant medicines such as Prozac, and tranquilizers such as Valium, these medications do not work for everyone. But a former NARSAD grantee and members of an international research team now report progress in understanding a new potential medical treatment for anxiety, which affects approximately 40 million American adults.

The researchers looked at the anxiety-reducing effects of oxytocin, a neurotransmitter sometimes called the "love hormone" for its ability to reduce stress and promote pro-social behaviors such as trust, empathy, and openness to social risk. Oxytocin has now been shown to make the amygdala less reactive to pictures of threatening or fearful faces. Previous research identified the amygdala as a crucial brain area for emotional processing.

https://bbrfoundation.org/brain-matters-discoveries/love-hormone-oxytocin-shows-promise-in-treating-anxiety-disorders

New Medications:

As we said in previous chapters; there are currently many different types of medications that can be utilized to treat anxiety (list of anxiolytics). The problem is that many of the drugs are poorly tolerated and/or produce significant unwanted side effects. Perhaps the most effective class of drugs to treat anxiety are the benzodiazepines as they provide rapid and significant relief.

The problem with the benzos is that they impair cognitive function while taking them, and long-term usage could lead to permanent memory impairment. (Read: Dementia linked to benzodiazepines). Ultimately most people end up better off (in terms of health) pursuing natural cures for anxiety such as taking up a meditation practice, partaking in cognitive behavioral therapy (CBT), reducing stress, and getting more exercise.

That said, there are people that have explored every logical method of biohacking their mental health and have still not been able to find relief. Sometimes people may genuinely need a medication to help them cope with their reality. Fortunately there are always new drugs on the horizon that give people who are struggling hope that one will be a "magic bullet."

In the United States, there are approximately 40 million people with anxiety disorders. Many of these individuals feel as if their anxiety is so bad, they can't work, talk, sleep, eat or function. If you happen to be struggling with significant anxiety, you may feel hopeful that there are new anxiolytics on the horizon that may be more effective and safer than older options.

MEDICINE#1

ALORADINE (PH94B)

This is a drug that has been in Phase III clinical trials since 2013 for the treatment of social anxiety disorder in women. It is being developed by the company Pherin Pharmaceuticals in the format of a "nasal spray." Of all the treatments for anxiety disorders in the pipeline, this one appears to have the most promise of actually making it to market.

What's unique about Aloradine is that it is a new class of treatments called "pherines." Pherines are compounds that directly influence targeted areas of the brain without circulating through the bloodstream to produce an effect. Aloradine is administered via nasal spray and is able to directly target peripheral receptors from "nasal chemosensory neurons" that are linked to the hypothalamus/limbic system of the brain. Its particular mechanism of action results in rapid relief from anxiety, and thus far it has been found to be both safe and very tolerable.

This "nasal spray" format may be favorable to antidepressant medications due to the fact that they often take weeks before a person experiences an anxiolytic effect. Even beta blockers for anxiety can take between 30 and 60 minutes before a person notices their full effect. With Aloradine, one spray can provide seemingly immediate relief. That said, I'm still not sure why the product is tailored specifically for women with anxiety.

The company developing this substance is known as Pherin Pharmaceuticals and focuses specifically on working with "pherins" to alter neuropsychiatric and neuroendocrine function within humans. They have other molecules in development for the treatment of depression, premenstrual dysphoria, and cognitive enhancement.

- Source: http://www.pherin.com/products.html
- Source: http://ajp.psychiatryonline.org/doi/abs/10.1176/appi.ajp.2014.12101342

MEDICINE#2

B-GOS

This is a prebiotic, or non-digestible food ingredients that improve healthy by stimulating the production of beneficial bacteria in the colon. It has long been thought that a person's gut flora (or bacteria) may play a role in determining whether they develop a mental illness or experience anxiety. Additionally, there is evidence demonstrating that most pharmaceutical drugs (e.g. antidepressants) have detrimental effects upon a person's gut flora.

Clasado Biosciences Limited currently are testing "B-GOS" in Phase I clinical trials. B-GOS is considered a unique "trans-galactooligosaccharide" and thus far has been shown to be effective in the reduction of anxiety. In preliminary research, it has been found to decrease both "waking cortisol levels" as well as "attentional vigilance towards negative information."

People who are overstimulated tend to have high levels of cortisol production, and often get caught up in negative thinking. It seems as though this prebiotic substance may provide some degree of relief. Early evidence also suggests that the substance may alter the functioning of the HPA (hypothalamic-pituitary-adrenal) axis. Individuals suffering from anxiety often have varying degrees of dysfunction within the HPA axis.

Some speculate that this substance may also prove to have therapeutic effects among individuals suffering from depression. There is mounting evidence that gut bacteria may be directly influencing brain function. Altering the gut microbiome may drastically change your mental health and/or cognition.

MEDICINE#3

IW-2143 (BNC210)

This is an experimental anxiolytic medication undergoing clinical trials, but there's currently no information regarding its mechanism of action. It has demonstrated a potent anxiolytic effect in animal subjects as well as in Phase I clinical trials. The good news is that it is unlikely to impair cognitive function, it isn't addictive (in rodent models), and won't make you feel sedated. No major side effects have been reported during the early stages of trials.

This drug is a "small molecule" that was discovered by the company Bionomics through a medicinal-chemistry program. Some evidence has shown that the molecule is capable of promoting "neurite" outgrowth (e.g. axon/dendrite). The company developing this drug (Bionomics) is a biotech company that is focused on creating therapies for CNS disorders. They have since licensed "BNC210" to Ironwood Pharmaceuticals, who refer to it as "IW-2143."

MEDICINE#4

S32212

This is a substance that is under investigation as a potential antidepressant with anxiolytic properties. It functions as a selective, inverse agonist at the 5-HT2C receptor, and Alpha-2 adrenergic receptor antagonist. It also elicits an effect upon the 5-HT2A receptor and a minimal one on the 5-HT2B receptor as an antagonist.

The good news is that it is thought to not affect histamine or acetylcholine receptors. Many drugs that affect H1 histamine and mACh receptors tend to result in memory impairment. Should this drug ever make it to the market, it will likely be classified as an NaSSA (noradrenergic and specific serotonergic antidepressant); the same classification of Remeron.

Based on animal research, this drug elevated levels of BDNF with the amygdala and hippocampus of the brain. It also amplified the amount of neuronal firing within other locations, while increasing neurotransmitters like norepinephrine, dopamine, and acetylcholine (in the prefrontal cortex). It didn't affect serotonin or histamine (which is probably a good thing).

Researchers have noted a variety of effects resulting from this substance including: antidepressant, anxiolytic, anti-obsessional, as well as anti-aggressive behaviors. It also is thought to enhance sleep and cognition in animals without any signs of weight fluctuation or diminished sex drive. Some speculate that it may even result in weight loss due to its "alpha blocking" effect.

MEDICINE#5

SL-651,498

This is a drug that has long been used as an anxiolytic in scientific research, but wasn't considered for human usage until 2006. In 2008, a report surfaced that preliminary human trials were underway and that the drug was considered as effective as Ativan in reducing anxiety, yet produced minimal sedation, cognitive impairment, or reduction in motor skills. This provides some early evidence that SL-651,498 may be an effective treatment.

Although its anxiolytic potential is equal to that of benzodiazepines, it is structurally distinct from the benzo classification. It has been classified as a "nonbenzodiazepine anxiolytic." It functions as a subtype-selective GABAA agonist, and elicits primarily anxiolytic effects in animals (with minor sedation). Early research has also suggested that the drug is unlikely to produce dependence or tolerance due to its low affinity for the Alpha-5 receptor.

From the little research there is, it appears as though this substance has some advantages over benzodiazepines. I'm not sure if we should buy into the lack of sedation and no cognitive impairment quite yet. Even if the cognitive impairment isn't "significant" in preliminary research, I wouldn't be surprised if it hampered cognition in later trials. In the coming years, we should get a better understanding of SL-651,498.

Which of these new anxiolytics seems most promising?

There really isn't enough data to compare these substances directly with one another to determine which is most promising. However, judging by the current statuses of each of the anxiolytics, it would appear as though Aloradine is a clear-cut favorite to get FDA approval simply because it is already in Phase III clinical trials. This doesn't mean that it will necessarily end up making it to the market, but it likely has something going for it to already be in Phase III.

Following Aloradine, I think the prebiotic B-GOS is relatively exciting because it highlights a new modality of treating anxiety. As science continues to decipher the functions of gut bacteria, more prebiotic treatments will likely surface as a means to influence brain function as well as physical health.

Personal thoughts on the new anxiolytics

I like the method of administration for Aloradine, reminds me of a natural substance called "Rescue Remedy" that works fast. I also like the fact that more attention is being paid to gut bacteria and its potential to cause anxiety. I don't think there are as many anxiolytics in development as there should be given the fact that the most effective drugs (e.g. benzos) are associated with addiction, dependence, and dementia.

When companies think outside the box to come up with unique treatments is what I like. The dogma that all cases of anxiety need to be treated with pills that target neurotransmitters can be put to rest. Unfortunately pharmaceutical companies have a tough time breaking free from the pill-to-target-a-specific-neurotransmitter paradigm. More attention needs to be paid to an individual from a holistic perspective rather than targeting one specific hormone, chemical, gut bacteria, etc.

There are an estimated 40 million people above age 18 that suffer from anxiety, while there are an estimated 350 million people that suffer from depression. Clearly more emphasis will be placed on coming up with treatments for the biggest societal burden that is depression. Fortunately with new research surfacing all the time of things that may be linked to anxiety (e.g. translocator protein), more companies should continue to improve upon existing treatments.

Are you excited about any new anxiolytics in development?

Although it could be the case that none of these anxiolytics ever make it through clinical trials, I have a hunch that some will. If you are excited about any anxiolytic in particular, feel free to share your thoughts in the comments section below. Keep in mind that none of these drugs should be perceived as a panacea and most will likely still carry side effects.

Some people may not be impressed at all by these developments in the works for anxiety, and that's fine. However, it's important to realize that we can all easily act as critics on the lack of new developments for the treatment of anxiety. If you want to improve treatments for mental illness, then you may want to consider contributing in whatever way you are capable to make it become a reality.

Modern research tools and techniques are giving scientists a more detailed understanding of the brain than ever before.

Using brain imaging technologies such as magnetic resonance imaging (MRI), which uses magnetic fields to take pictures of the brain's structure, studies show that brain growth in children with autism appears to peak early. And as they grow there are differences in brain development in children who develop bipolar disorder than children who do not. Studies comparing such children to those with normal brain development may help scientists to pinpoint when and where mental disorders begin and perhaps how to slow or stop them from progressing. Functional magnetic resonance imaging (fMRI) is another important research tool in understanding how the brain functions.

Another type of brain scan called magnetoencephalography, or MEG, can capture split-second changes in the brain. Using MEG, some scientists have found a specific pattern of brain activity that may help predict who is most likely to respond to fast-acting antidepressant medications. Currently available antidepressants usually take four to six weeks to reach their full effect, which can be a difficult wait for some people struggling with depression. However, recent research points to a possible new class of antidepressants that can relieve symptoms of the illness in just a few hours. Knowing who might respond to such medications could reduce the amount of trial and error and frustration that many people with depression experience when starting treatment.

Advanced technologies are also making it faster, easier, and more affordable to study genes. Scientists have found many different genes and groups of genes that appear to increase risk or provide protection from various mental disorders. Other genes may change the way a person responds to a certain medication. This information may someday make it possible to predict who will develop a mental disorder and to tailor the treatment for a person's specific conditions.

Such brain research help increase the understanding of how the brain grows and works and the effects of genes and environment on mental health. This knowledge is allowing scientists to make important discoveries that could change the way we think about and treat mental illnesses.

The National Institute of Mental Health supports many studies on mental health and the brain. You can read about some of these studies online at www.nimh.nih.gov.

I added some summary of the most important papers I consider about the future of GAD treatments.

PAPER#1

Mystery Gene Reveals New Mechanism for Anxiety Disorders

Researchers have linked seven new genes to anxiety disorders such as obsessive compulsive disorder, panic disorder and social anxiety disorder.

These gene links mean that new drug treatments could be created to target these gene products specifically in the treatment of anxiety disorders. It gives hope to thousands of people who currently have no treatment plan.

Treatments for anxiety disorders involve both drug-free and drug-based therapies. The most effective treatment strategies are a combination of the two, differing in application from patient to patient.

To treat these conditions using drug-based therapies, drugs have been designed to target specific genes which produce proteins associated with the progression of disorders. Because these disorders are so complex, gene discovery is difficult.

Currently, there are only two core pathways that are associated with drug-based therapies: the dopaminergic and the serotonergic pathways. Dopamine changes have been linked to movement, motivation, reward-response and addiction. Serotonin in the brain has been linked to mood, social behaviour, memory and cognitive function.

Drug-based therapies work on roughly half of those affected and treated, leaving a large number of people without tangible assistance. The current treatments for anxiety disorders are not as effective as hoped. A better understanding of why and how these disorders exist is essential for better treatment strategies.

PAPER#2

Mystery Link between metabolic system and brain activity suggests new treatment targets

May 15, 2012

A novel mechanism for anxiety behaviors, including a previously unrecognized inhibitory brain signal, may inspire new strategies for treating psychiatric disorders, University of Chicago researchers report.

By testing the controversial role of a gene called Glo1 in anxiety, scientists uncovered a new inhibitory factor in the brain: the metabolic by-product methylglyoxal. The system offers a tantalizing new target for drugs designed to treat conditions such as anxiety disorder, epilepsy, and sleep disorders.

The study, published in the *Journal of Clinical Investigation*, found that animals with multiple copies of the Glo1 gene were more likely to exhibit anxiety-like behavior in laboratory tests. Further experiments showed that Glo1 increased anxiety-like behavior by lowering levels of methylglyoxal (MG). Conversely, inhibiting Glo1 or raising MG levels reduced anxiety behaviors.

"Animals transgenic for Glo1 had different levels of anxiety-like behavior, and more copies made them more anxious," said Abraham Palmer, PhD, assistant professor of human genetics at the University of Chicago Medicine and senior author of the study. "We showed that Glo1 was causally related to anxiety-like behavior, rather than merely correlated."

In 2005, a comparison of different mouse strains found a link between anxiety-like behaviors and Glo1, the gene encoding the metabolic enzyme glyoxylase 1. However, subsequent studies questioned the link, and the lack of an obvious connection between glyoxylase 1 and brain function or behavior made some scientists skeptical.

"When people discover a gene, they're always most comfortable when they discover something they already knew," Palmer said. "The alarming thing here was there was a discovery of something that nobody knew, and therefore it seemed less likely to actually be correct."

A 2009 study from Palmer's laboratory suggested that differences in Glo1 expression between mouse strains were due to copy number variants, where the segment of the genome containing the gene is repeated multiple times. To test this hypothesis, lead author Margaret Distler inserted two, eight or ten copies of the Glo1 gene into mouse lines. She then ran experiments such as the open field test, in which researchers measure how much time a mouse spends in the center of an arena versus along the walls, to detect changes in anxiety behavior.

The results confirmed a causative role for Glo1 copy number variants, as mice with more copies of the Glo1 gene exhibited higher anxiety-like behavior in their experiments.

"It's the first study to show that it's the copy number variant that has the potential to change Glo1 expression and behavior," said Distler, an MD/PhD student in the Pritzker School of Medicine's Medical Scientist Training Program. "Our study was a physiological representation of what it means to increase Glo1 expression for anxiety."

The researchers then set about answering the mystery of how Glo1 expression influences anxiety-like behaviors. The primary function of glyoxylase 1 is to metabolize and lower cellular levels of methylglyoxal, a waste product of glycolysis. Distler produced the opposite effect by injecting MG to artificially increase its levels in the brain, finding that raising MG levels quickly reduced anxiety symptoms in mice.

"Methylglyoxal changed behavior within 10 minutes of administration, which means it's a rapid onset. It's not changing gene expression, and it's not having long-term downstream effects," Distler said. "That was our first breakthrough."

The short time course suggested that MG might have a direct effect on neuronal activity. MG also demonstrated sedative effects at high doses, a hallmark of drugs that activate inhibitory GABA receptors on neurons. In collaboration with Leigh Plant, now at Brandeis University, the researchers demonstrated that MG activated GABA-A receptors on neurons, a previously unknown inhibitory mechanism.

"It's a completely different system that is tying neuronal inhibitory tone into metabolic activity," Palmer said. "That's potentially really exciting in terms of re-evaluating what we thought we knew about inhibitory tone in the CNS. It turns out now that methylglyoxal, which has been around ever since glycolysis evolved, was also acting at these receptors, and nobody knew that."

Conventionally, anxiety has been treated with drugs that activate the GABA-A receptor, such as benzodiazepines and barbiturates, which are prone to abuse and dangerous side effects. The researchers theorized that targeting the Glo1/MG interaction could provide a more selective strategy for reducing anxiety symptoms by subtly influencing inhibitory tone.

"The GABA-A receptor agents already out there have a lot of side effects, such as sedation and hypothermia, as well as a high abuse liability," Distler said. "It's possible that taking a Glo1 inhibitor will increase only MG levels to a certain maximum. You could have the potential for more specificity, given that you're activating a system that's already in place, not just dumping methylglyoxal or some other GABA-A receptor agent throughout the brain."

Preliminary experiments with a small molecule inhibitor of Glo1 supported the theory. Injections of the inhibitor, developed by John Termini at the Beckman Research Institute of the City of Hope, reduced anxiety-like symptoms in mice.

"It's a different way of hitting these GABA-A receptors," Palmer said. "We have yet to determine if that's a better way of doing it, but it's certainly different, and it gives us a unique angle of attack on this system and potential advantages that we have yet to evaluate."

Such a drug may also be useful in treating epilepsy and sleep disorders, where GABA-A drugs have shown success. While the therapeutic potential of manipulating this system is yet to be determined, the research clears the fog around the role of Glo1 in anxiety by adding behavioral and cellular evidence.

"What's neat is that we started with exploratory, open-ended genetic studies in mice, and we've now gotten into some fundamental new physiology that nobody had appreciated or put together before," Palmer said. "Now we're starting to reap some of the fruit from those types of genetic studies to enrich our understanding of more classical aspects of biology."

The paper, "Glyoxalase 1 increases anxiety by reducing GABAA receptor agonist methylglyoxal," will be published online May 15 by the *Journal of Clinical Investigation*. In addition to Distler, Palmer, Plant and Termini, authors on the paper include Greta Sokoloff, Andrew Hawk, Ivy Aneas, Stephen Meredith and Marcelo Nobrega of the University of Chicago, and Gerald Wuenschell of the Beckman Research Institute of the City of Hope.

The research was funded by grants from the National Institute of Mental Health, the National Institute on Drug Abuse, National Institute of General Medical Sciences and the University of Chicago Diabetes Research and Training Center.

The University of Chicago Medicine
Communications
950 E. 61st Street, Third Floor
Chicago, IL 60637
Phone (773) 702-0025 Fax (773) 702-3171

PAPER#3

Current Diagnosis and Treatment of Anxiety Disorders

Alexander Bystritsky, MD, PhD, Sahib S. Khalsa, MD, PhD, Michael E. Cameron, PhD, and Jason Schiffman, MD, MA, MBA
Author information ▶ Article notes ▶ Copyright and License information ▶
This article has been cited by other articles in PMC.
Go to:

Abstract

Anxiety disorders are the most prevalent mental health conditions. Although they are less visible than schizophrenia, depression, and bipolar disorder, they can be just as disabling. The diagnoses of anxiety disorders are being continuously revised. Both dimensional and structural diagnoses have been used in clinical treatment and research, and both methods have been proposed for the new classification in the *Diagnostic and Statistical Manual of Mental Disorders IV (DSM-5)*. However, each of these approaches has limitations. More recently, the emphasis in diagnosis has focused on neuroimaging and genetic research. This approach is based partly on the need for a more comprehensive understanding of how biology, stress, and genetics interact to shape the symptoms of anxiety.

Anxiety disorders can be effectively treated with psychopharmacological and cognitive–behavioral interventions. These interventions have different symptom targets; thus, logical combinations of these strategies need to be further studied in order to improve future outcomes. New developments are forthcoming in the field of alternative strategies for managing anxiety and for treatment-resistant cases. Additional treatment enhancements should include the development of algorithms that can be easily used in primary care and with greater focus on managing functional impairment in patients with anxiety.

Within the past 10 years or so, epidemiological data have been used in the attempt to refine the boundaries of diagnostic categories of anxiety disorders. The results of this approach have been progressively reflected from *DSM III* to *IIIR* to *DSM IV-TR* and, finally, to *DSM-5*. However, this effort has been hampered by the extensive presence of comorbidities in patients with anxiety, as revealed by the National Comorbidity Survey (NCS). For instance, in patients with some disorders such as generalized anxiety disorder (GAD) and social anxiety disorder (SAD), the presence of comorbidities is a rule rather than the exception.[2] In clinical practice and in research, it is not unusual to find the coexistence of two or more diagnosable conditions in the same patient or at least symptomatic overlap with several subsyndromal states. This is particularly true for symptom overlap between different anxiety disorders, depression, and alcohol and drug abuse.

A related phenomenon is the emergence of different disorders in the same patient over a lifetime. For example, during an initial evaluation, the original diagnosis could be panic disorder that resolves after treatment, and then presents after a few years with symptoms more suitable to a diagnosis of OCD or GAD. Whether this process reflects a primary diathesis or two distinct entities is uncertain.

Another significant problem with the present classification of anxiety disorders is the absence of known etiological factors and of specific treatments for different diagnostic categories. Studying the genetic underpinnings of anxiety disorders using molecular biological techniques has failed to produce a single gene or a cluster of genes implicated as an etiologic factor for any single anxiety disorder, even though some genetic findings exist for OCD and panic disorder. Despite a lack of specificity, family and twin studies point to the importance of genetic factors that are possibly shared among various anxiety disorders, depression, and alcohol and drug abuse.

Despite these diagnostic ambiguities, the emergence of efficacious serotonergic medications that cut across a variety of categorical disorders (e.g., mood and anxiety) has led many to suggest that a dimensional model might be more applicable in the study and treatment of these conditions. In this view, the disorder is seen as a complex set of coexisting symptom dimensions (e.g., panic, social awkwardness, and obsessiveness). Each of these dimensions can vary, depending on hypothetical, biological, or genetic factors, which may dictate separate biological or psychological treatment approaches.[9] The usefulness of the dimensional versus the categorical approach remains a highly debatable topic in research and in clinical practice and is one of the bases for the introduction of *DSM-5*.

Within psychiatry, similarities between distinct disorders has led to the emergence of the term "spectrum" disorders, a concept initially developed for OCD. This conceptualization was helpful in evaluating similar responses to pharmacological and psychological treatments and has been expanded to consider many other spectra such as social anxiety, panic–agoraphobia, and post-traumatic disorders. This approach, although useful, can be overly inclusive and misleading because it sometimes lumps together disorders that have little in common, such as placing pathological gambling and body dysmorphic disorder (BDD) in the same OCD spectrum. So far, few genetic or neuro-circuitry investigations have validated this concept.

Dimensional and categorical diagnosis in the *DSM-IV-TR* is usually produced by cross-sectional comparisons of distinct subject samples. However, diagnostic presentations in clinical practice occur in individuals treated sequentially and may therefore be better understood as part of a psychopathological process that unfolds over time. For example, although a patient might meet criteria for OCD purely on the basis of obsessions or compulsions, the latter usually arise later in the disorder as if to counteract the threat and anxiety associated with obsessive thoughts.

Analogous viewpoints can be found in medical disease, with symptoms usually representing a combination of a noxious agent and the body's reaction to its presence. For instance, when the lungs are infected with the harmful organism *Mycobacterium tuberculosis*, they compensate by forming scars around the tissue. In the short run, this may be effective in walling off the infection (and may even elude clinical detection), but the strategy fails when pushed to the extreme, leading to respiratory compromise in some cases.

In recent years, scientists and clinicians have begun to realize that the processes underlying anxiety and fear might be similar among the various disorders. This has resulted in the implementation of uniform treatment regimens in primary care and in the development of the unified theory of anxiety.

United States Mental Health System.

The mental health-care system in the United States is a multibillion-dollar industry; but that is still not big enough to serve all those who need it. The Budget can't cover what is needed. The United States spends $113 billion on mental health treatment. That works out to about 5.6 percent of the national health-care spending, according to a 2011 paper in the journal Health Affairs. This puts us in the same range as other developed nations including Australia and Italy, according to the World Health Organization. Egypt leads the group of countries they surveyed, spending 9 percent of its health budget on mental health treatment. Mental health dollars mostly go toward prescription drugs and outpatient treatment.

In the 60's mental health in US was treated mostly for inpatient cold institutions so an inpatient program was put in place. But in the decades since, the sickest patients have begun turning up in jails and homeless shelters with a frequency that mirrors that of the late 1800s. "We're protecting civil liberties at the expense of health and safety," says Doris A. Fuller, the executive director of the Treatment Advocacy Center, a nonprofit group that lobbies for broader involuntary commitment standards. "Deinstitutionalization has gone way too far."

Access to mental health care is worse than other types of medical services. The Bureau of Labor Statistics estimated in 2010 that the country had 156,300 mental health counselors. Access to mental health professionals is worse than for other types of doctors: 89.3 million Americans live in federally-designated Mental Health Professional Shortage Areas, compared to 55.3 million Americans living in similarly-designated primary-care shortage areas and 44.6 million in dental health shortage areas. **Mental health care is pricey, with 45 percent of the untreated citing cost as a barrier.** A quarter of the 15.7 million Americans who received mental health care listed themselves as the main payer for the services, according to one survey that looked at those services from 2005 to 2009. The majority of those who did seek outpatient treatment had out-of-pocket costs between $100 and $5,000.

These findings suggest that even though the majority of adults have some form of health insurance coverage, there are significant limitations on coverage for mental health services," federal researchers wrote in a July 2011 brief. Separate research from the same agency found 45 percent of those not receiving mental health care listing cost as a barrier. It's worth noting though that Americans actually pick up a larger percent of the tab for their physical health-care costs than for mental health-care services. Americans paid 13 percent of the costs for health-care services generally in 2005, compared to 11 percent of behavioral health spending, which includes both mental health and substance abuse treatment.

Attitudes about mental health services are another big barrier to care. A 2007 study in the journal Psychiatric Services looked at 303 mental health patients who had, in the past year, thought about going to the doctor but decided against it. The researchers asked them why. The most frequent response, from 66 percent of the patients, had to do with attitude: They thought the problem would get better on its own.

Seventy-one percent agreed with the statement "I wanted to solve the problem on my own."

Cost was a barrier too: 47 percent cited financial obstacles as a reason not to seek treatment. Still, attitudinal barriers about the value of mental health care seemed to be be the biggest obstacle. **States cut $1.8 billion from their mental health budgets during the recession.** That figure comes from the National Alliance on Mental Illness, which notes that states tend to play a larger role in providing mental health services than they do with physical health.

That means that much of the treatment of the mentally ill shifts toward other places in the health-care system. The NAMI report looks at Rhode Island, which has seen a "a 65 percent increase in the number of children living with mental illness boarding in public emergency rooms" after a series of budget cuts.

Recent federal legislation requires more expansive insurance coverage for mental health services. The Mental Health Parity and Addiction Act of 2008 applies to large, employer-sponsored insurance plans. It bars insurers from putting up financial barriers to mental health care that are greater than those created for physical treatments. While there was some concern that the new requirements would lead employers to drop mental health coverage altogether, a poll by the Kaiser Family Foundation found only 2 percent did so.

The Affordable Care Act creates more mental health mandates, by requiring all insurers who sell on the exchanges to include such treatments in their benefit packages. Under the ACA, insurers are for the first time required to cover mental health and substance abuse treatment as one of ten "essential benefits." This is good news for the millions of Americans who suffer from some form of mental illness but don't seek treatment. The question now is whether the country's mental health infrastructure is equipped to deal with an avalanche of new patients. The answer? Probably not.

Mental health care is saddled with two problems: It's expensive and inaccessible. A 2012 survey by the Substance Abuse and Mental Health Services Administration found that more than 18 percent of American adults suffered from some form of mental illness in the past year. Of the forty percent who sought treatment, more than one-third paid for it out-of-pocket. To put this in perspective, only about 16 percent of health care consumers overall pay for services out-of-pocket. Cost is the number-one reason why millions of Americans with mental illness forgo medical care.

Despite the high price tag, the demand for mental health care far exceeds the supply of mental health providers. This is largely due to a growing shortage of psychiatrists. According to the Association of American Medical Colleges, the number of licensed psychiatrists dropped slightly between 2005 and 2010, while the general population grew nearly five percent. An alarming 57 percent of psychiatrists are over the age of 55, with retirement on the horizon. It's no wonder that in most parts of the country, wait times to see a psychiatrist hover in the weeks and months, not days.

Coaxing more psychiatrists out of medical schools will be no easy task. Students who want a high-paying job generally don't turn to psychiatry; the median income for a psychiatrist is hundreds of thousands of dollars less than the salary for a surgeon or anesthesiologist. But money isn't the only reason why med students are turning up their nose at the specialty. Beginning with Sigmund Freud, psychiatrists used to emphasize talk therapy. The rise of big pharma changed all that. Insurance companies pay twice as much for a medication consultation than for a traditional therapy session. Now, many psychiatrists spend their days scribbling cocktails of anti-depressants and anti-anxiety medicines on prescription pads during 15-minute consultations.

The Affordable Care Act tackles one element of this problem by requiring all insurance companies to cover mental health and addiction care. In the past, insurers might have wormed their way around this constraint by charging a higher co-pay for psychiatrist visits or refusing to cover them entirely. The wily architects of the ACA preempted this with a new "parity" rule; insurers must cover mental illness like any other condition, whether it's epilepsy or cancer. This should, at least in theory, make mental health care affordable.

But the ACA is far from a panacea. The dearth of psychiatrists means that a small number of providers will face a deluge of new patients, many of whom could not have afforded insurance before. Although psychiatry is often considered to be a profession that caters to elites (Woody Allen rambling about his childhood memories in Annie Hall) people living in poverty are disproportionately likely to need psychiatric care—and the least likely to get it. Psychiatrists are overwhelmingly concentrated in urban areas, and many operate in solo practice, performing administrative tasks themselves. The stiff competition to get into a psychiatrist's office, combined with the hassle of filing insurance paperwork, may undermine one of the ACA's fundamental goals: bringing mental health care to low-income patients.

For example, the new parity requirement won't make a difference if your psychiatrist doesn't take insurance to begin with. Dr. Tara Bishop, an assistant professor of public health and medicine at Weill Cornell Medical College, surveyed psychiatrists and discovered that only 55 percent accept insurance, compared to 89 percent of other doctors. One of the reasons, Bishop speculates, may be the complexity of the reimbursement process. For a psychiatrist in a solo practice, it might not make sense to spend hours every week exchanging forms with insurance companies. The dearth of colleagues makes it easy for psychiatrists to fill their appointment calendars with patients who can pay full price.

Finding a psychiatrist who takes Medicaid is an even knottier task. Bishop found that only 43 percent of psychiatrists take Medicaid. Another study, conducted by researchers from Emory and the University of California-San Francisco, found that mental health providers are especially scarce in rural areas with large low-income, minority populations. Most psychiatrists who accept Medicaid work in outpatient clinics or community mental health facilities, but one-third of counties have no such provider. So even in the states that opt in to Medicaid expansion—giving a wider swath of people access to insurance—there won't be anywhere near enough doctors to cope.

Janet Cummings, an assistant professor of health policy at Emory University and one of the study's co-authors, says that tele-psychiatry is one of the easiest ways to bring mental health care into rural parts of the country. Most counties, whether or not they have a psychiatrist who takes Medicaid, have a federally-funded community health clinic that could establish partnerships with hospitals in big cities. With the right equipment, patients could visit their local clinic and teleconference with a doctor miles away. The problem, Cummings says, is that most clinics don't have the technology for these kinds of consultations—and it's expensive. Part of the ACA's funding is earmarked for telemedicine expansions, but it's far from enough to address the existing need. Some insurance companies are starting to get in the game, though; last year, CareFirst BlueCross BlueShield announced that it would invest $1.5 million in telemedicine grants for behavioral health providers.

Most of these problems aren't unique to the mental health system, which might actually make them easier to solve. Primary care physicians are also underequipped for a deluge of new patients (although there's a much better chance they'll take your insurance). The remedy isn't just to entice more medical students into psychiatry and family medicine. Instead, community clinics and hospitals should make better use of their nurse practitioners and social workers to ensure, in health care reformers' argot, that everyone is working at the "top of their license."

For example, there's no medical reason why psychiatrists, once they've decided on a particular treatment for a patient, shouldn't delegate responsibility for refills to a nurse. This notion should make sense to anyone who's paid a $50 for a routine visit to the psychiatrist, only to exchange small talk for ten minutes and walk out with a prescription.

This could result in a system where mental health and primary care overlap more than they currently do. "People with mental health problems often have another illness that isn't being adequately treated," says Chuck Ingoglia, a senior vice president at the National Council for Behavioral Health. "We want all of the staff at health clinics to pay attention to mental health conditions and symptoms but also be able to educate and engage clients about other health needs."

The Future of Mental Help.

Let's start with Genetics and Neurobiology. For me this is the near future for treatment of Bipolar Disorder, Anxiety, and more.

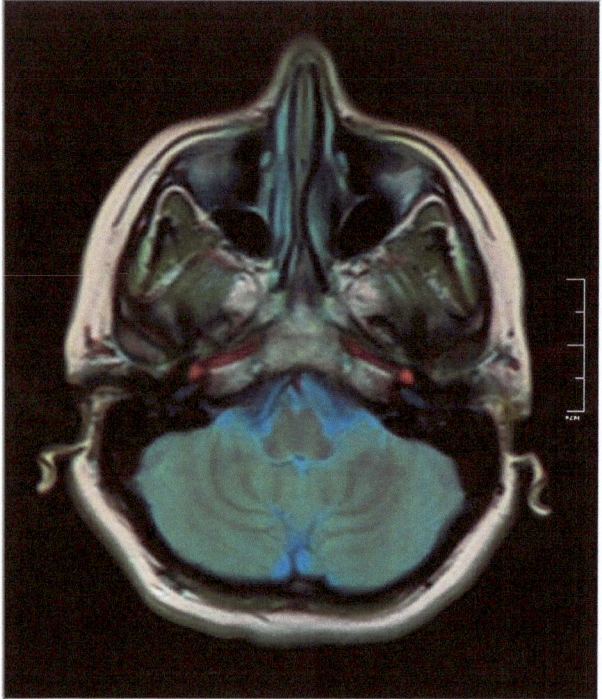

Fig 11

Patients with **bipolar disorder** experience recurrent episodes of mood disturbance, ranging from extreme elation (mania) to severe depression.

Bipolar disorder is currently diagnosed on the basis of clinical symptoms, such as alternating periods of depression and mania. The contribution of environmental and social factors toward an individual's risk of developing bipolar disorder should not be underestimated, yet studies of families and twins show the importance of genetic factors affecting susceptibility to bipolar disorder. Scientists' growing knowledge of the contribution of genetics to bipolar disorder nonetheless leads to the tantalizing possibility that scientists might be on the verge of being able to identify some of the biological systems that lead to illness in bipolar disorder, which could in turn lead to substantial improvements in diagnosis and treatment of the illness.

"The association between genotype and phenotype for psychiatric disorders is clearly complex. The key point is that most cases of bipolar disorder involve the interplay of several genes or more complex genetic mechanisms, together with the effects of the environment, and chance.
Bipolar disorder research now needs to follow up genetic studies with imaging and psychological studies in order to try and unravel the complex biological mechanisms involved in bipolar disorder, and bring biological understanding closer to the experience of the patient.

Substantial difficulties complicate the diagnosis of bipolar disorder, which refers to a group of affective disorders. These affective disorders include bipolar disorder type I (depressive and manic episodes: this disorder can be diagnosed on the basis of one manic episode), bipolar disorder type II (depressive and hypomanic episodes), cyclothymic disorder (hypomanic and depressive symptoms that do not meet criteria for depressive episodes), and bipolar disorder not otherwise specified (depressive and hypomanic-like symptoms that do not meet the diagnostic criteria for any of the aforementioned disorders).

Depressive symptoms are considerably more prevalent than manic symptoms over the course of the illness for most people with bipolar disorder, and people are more likely to seek treatment for depressive symptoms. There is an average delay of five to 10 years between the onset of bipolar disorder and diagnosis, and misdiagnosis of the disorder as unipolar depression is common. Most importantly, the medicine for unipolar depression could exacerbate the manic symptoms.

"Identifying objective biomarkers that differ between bipolar and unipolar depression would not only lead to more accurate diagnosis but potentially to new, personalized treatments, yet very little research has been undertaken in this area,For instance, very few neuroimaging studies have been done in which the brains of people with bipolar disorder have been compared to those of people with unipolar disorder, and further research into this area is urgently needed.
Lithium, first introduced in 1949, remains the best long-term treatment for bipolar disorder, but its benefits are restricted and alternatives are often needed for lengthy treatment. There have been no fundamental advances in the search for more effective treatment for bipolar disorder in the last 20 years. "Combining psychosocial treatments - which can include not just psychotherapy for the patient, but family therapy involving education for their family or caregiver - with mood stabilising drugs might well be one of the most promising lines of treatment for bipolar disorder.
Treating bipolar is complex because the same treatments that alleviate depression can cause mania or mood swings, and treatments that reduce mania may cause rebound depressive episodes. The development of future treatments should consider both the neurobiological and psychosocial mechanisms underlying the disorder.

Brain & Behavior Research Foundation Scientific Council Member, Dr. Husseini Manji, is one of the leading contemporary explorers of the brain — that remarkable 3-pound organ

which he reminds us is "the very basis of human society and civilization" — so complex and capable, yet so delicate and vulnerable.

What he calls the "exquisite inner balances" that enable our brains to work efficiently are in various ways disturbed in brain and behavior disorders. But, he stresses, "our research is showing us something that fills us with hope. We now have reason to believe that we can use the brain's own biological assets — its inherent plasticity — to help restore that balance in a number of disorders."

"For complex brain illnesses," he states, "it will not be a question of finding the magic bullet that will make life fine. It is important to 'think beyond the pill.' It's going to take what I call a holistic solution." He explains, "Some of that may involve drug-device combinations; some of the future treatments will be neurotrophic — that is, they will help nerve cells restore their health or allow them to grow and communicate better. But you can't think of that like 'brain fertilizer' that you can sprinkle over the brain and hope for the best." Dr. Manji insists that it's necessary to "activate specific circuits upon which the brain's self-nurturing and self-repairing capacities can act."

Is now believe Bipolar, isn't a disease of too much or too little serotonin or dopamine. It is not about the 'chemical soup' of neurotransmitters in the brain, but rather it is about synaptic and neural plasticity."

Plasticity is the attribute that enables the billions of nerve cells in the brain to change and adapt on a millisecond-by-millisecond basis in response to the many inputs that are continually being processed. What we've learned in the last 10 years is that whether we're talking about memory or mood or movement, all advanced brain functions involve changes in the ability to convey information between synapses in different circuits.

Rather than too much of this neurochemical or too little of that one, we now think of the problem as being in the machinery of signal transmission. Not only is this machinery engaged in information processing; the same machinery seems also to be involved in helping nerve cells survive and grow.

While there is atrophy or shrinkage of neurons in certain brain areas in individuals with mood disorders, the neurons are not dead. Neurons normally have a profusion of tree-like branches, and they communicate with one another by forming a multitude of synapses between these branches. Synapses are tiny gaps across which the neuron that is sending information transmits signals to the neuron that is receiving it. If that branch shrivels up, you lose synaptic contacts, And how can you expect to have communication when that happens?

Dr. Manji and others helped demonstrate in the 1990s that the drug lithium, which is the oldest and most successful mood-stabilizer for bipolar disorder, has "neuroprotective" effects. The discovery that it boosts levels of proteins that help neurons maintain their function and other proteins that help neurons and their treelike branches grow seems to explain the fact that lithium is effective over long periods of time. It doesn't, in other words, simply address a short-term problem but contributes to the long-term maintenance of the machinery within nerve cells that enables signals to pass properly from one cell to the next.

Not only did the discovery of lithium's neuroprotective qualities help explain resilience; it also provided plausible answers to another mystery. "The plasticity that the drug revealed also helped us theorize why it might take several weeks for SSRI antidepressant drugs to take effect," says Dr. Manji. People with bipolar disorder provided vivid proof that depression can rapidly cease. "If a bipolar patient is sleep-deprived, for example, they can go from depression to mania literally overnight. Other patients spontaneously flip from one polarity of mood to the other. This suggests that maybe our antidepressant drugs don't work rapidly because they are going after the wrong target!"

The drugs, in other words, [antidepressants] address the balance of neurotransmitters, while the real anti-depressant action might come from modifying synaptic plasticity. This was an interesting hypothesis, but the idea generated greater excitement when ketamine, an agent long used as an anesthetic, was given to people with severe depression. In many cases, the depression melted away in a few hours.

Understanding how this might be possible has shed further light on how better to control the symptoms of bipolar disorder and MDD. "One of the major mechanisms by which neurons bring about plasticity is that they move things called AMPA and NMDA receptors into and out of certain synapses," says Dr. Manji. "This has the effect of making the connection between nerve cells stronger or weaker."

"Research suggests that you want to increase the AMPA type or reduce the NMDA type of receptors in specific synapses to treat MDD. It happens that ketamine blocks NMDA receptors." Once this was demonstrated, Dr. Manji and others conducted trials in which ketamine was given to severely depressed patients who had failed other forms of treatment, including antidepressants and electroconvulsive therapy (ECT). "It was remarkable—people who had failed six different drugs and also ECT and had been continuously depressed for 3 years started to respond within two hours. Within 24 hours, 70% had responded to the ketamine."

Ketamine is a controversial treatment not currently approved by the FDA, in part because of its potential side effects, which can include hallucinations and dissociation (feeling "unreal" for brief periods). But as a research tool, it has raised hopes. According to Dr. Manji, a single infusion of low-dose ketamine (much lower than used in anesthesia), given over 40 minutes, continues to show therapeutic antidepressant effects a week and sometimes two weeks later, long after the drug has left the body. In small studies, it has also proved surprisingly effective as an agent to reduce suicidal thinking. As with all experimental treatments, more work is needed to validate its use in non-research settings.

Dr. Manji and others now look for other ways of doing what ketamine does; agents that "will enable us to fine-tune the balance between the AMPA and NMDA receptors." He notes that pioneering treatments by his colleagues on the **Scientific Council**, Dr. Helen Mayberg, and separately, Dr. Fritz Henn, have also suggested that there may be ways to "switch" severe depression "off" in very short order. Drs. Mayberg and Henn have used precisely targeted electrical stimulation delivered via surgically implanted probes to rapidly reverse refractory depression in a limited number of clinical trial patients. Dr. Manji notes that Area 25, which Dr. Mayberg and colleagues have pinpointed, happens to be a brain region rich in NMDA receptors.

The research goes forward. Piecing together new knowledge gained over the last decade, Dr. Manji offers this metaphoric account of what goes wrong in bipolar disorder. "We think that in bipolar disorder, one of the problems is that a very finely-tuned system, almost like a thermostat, is faulty. When a person with MDD is coming out of a depressive episode, the cellular thermostat should and does prevent mood from 'overshooting' in the other direction. But in bipolar disorder, the thermostat inside the nerve cell is sluggish, it is not well-tuned, and so when you come out of your depression, you overshoot over to the manic side of the mood continuum."

Scientists don't yet have enough factual data to prove this hypothesis, but Dr. Manji is adamant about the importance of it not being overwhelming. Rather than thinking of fixing all dysfunctions with new pills, Dr. Manji suggests we keep our focus on moving toward the notion of harnessing the brain's own capacities for plasticity and restoration: "Not, 'let's block this receptor,' but 'could we use this capacity that nerve cells already have — could we activate it in a person with bipolar disorder in whom the program has been shut down or is somehow broken?" He concludes, "We don't need to know everything about the brain to arrive at better treatments," he says. "I believe our recently gained knowledge is moving us close to some important improvements."

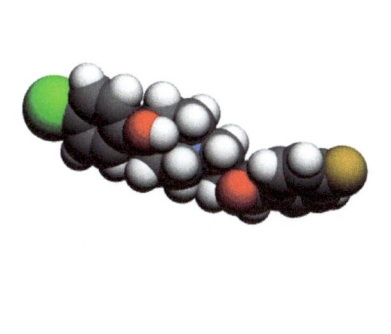

The spinning molecule above is haloperidol, a first generation antipsychotic drug developed in 1958 and approved by the FDA in 1967 as a treatment for schizophrenia. It's a dopamine blocker known for producing untoward extrapyramidal side effects, or movement disorders such as tremors and tardive dyskinesia. Nonetheless, haloperidol (Haldol®) is still the most effective drug for the acute treatment of mania, and fairly well tolerated (see HAL in the figure below). The second generation (atypical) antipsychotics risperidone(RIS) and olanzapine (OLZ) also turn out pretty well in the antimanic sweepstakes. But these drugs can also have untoward side effects, notably substantial weight gain that can lead to high cholesterol, diabetes, and metabolic syndrome.

Overall, advances in drug treatment remain quite modest. Antipsychotic drugs are effective in the acute treatment of mania; their efficacy in the treatment of depression is variable with the clearest evidence for quetiapine. Despite their widespread use, considerable uncertainty and controversy remains about the use of antidepressant drugs in the management of depressive episodes. Lithium has the strongest evidence for long-term relapse prevention; the evidence for anticonvulsants such as divalproex and lamotrigine is less robust and there is much uncertainty about the longer term benefits of antipsychotics.

Fig 12

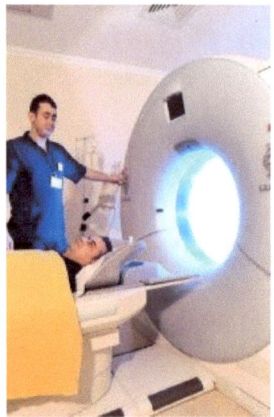

Fig 13

Using magnetic resonance imaging (MRI) may be an effective way to diagnose mental illnesses, such as bipolar disorder, according to new research.

In a new study, researchers from the Icahn School of Medicine at Mount Sinai were able to correctly distinguish bipolar patients from healthy individuals based on their brain scans alone most, but not all, of the time.

"Bipolar disorder affects patients' ability to regulate their emotions successfully, which puts them at great disadvantage in their lives," said Sophia Frangou, professor of psychiatry at Mount Sinai Hospital in New York.

"The situation is made worse by unacceptably long delays, sometimes of up to 10 years, in making the correct diagnosis. Bipolar disorder may be easily misdiagnosed for other disorders, such as depression or schizophrenia."

Frangou said that is why bipolar disorder ranks among the top 10 disorders worldwide in terms of significant disability.

Frangou and her team used MRI to scan the brains of people with bipolar disorder and of healthy individuals. Using advanced computational models, they were successful in

References.

1. http://www.dsm5.org/Research/Documents/Andrews%20et%20al_Generalized%20Worry%20Disorder.pdf

2. https://www.sciencedaily.com/releases/2009/12/091207164850.htm

3. http://research.labiomed.org/Biostat/Education/CaseStudies2008/Session5/PollackJClinPsy2005.pdf

4. https://en.wikipedia.org/wiki/Gamma-Aminobutyric_acid

5. https://www.shodor.org/unchem/basic/nomen/index.html

6. http://www.brainphysics.com/howprozacworks.php

7. http://www.drugs.com/sfx/prozac-side-effects.html

8. http://www.nimh.nih.gov/health/educational-resources/brain-basics/brain-basics.shtml

9. http://www.medscape.com/viewarticle/431268

10. http://www.uchospitals.edu/news/2012/20120515-anxiety-disorders.html

11. http://www.ncbi.nlm.nih.gov/pmc/articles/PMC3628173/

12. http://www.mayoclinic.org/diseases-conditions/generalized-anxiety-disorder/basics/treatment/con-20024562

13. http://www.forensic-psych.com/articles/artBenzo.php

14. http://patienttimes.com/twelve-problems-with-benzodiazepines/

15. https://www.washingtonpost.com/news/wonk/wp/2012/12/17/seven-facts-about-americas-mental-health-care-system/

16. http://prospect.org/article/aca-cant-fix-our-mental-health-crisis

17. http://www.medicaldaily.com/genetics-and-neurobiology-future-bipolar-disorder-treatment-and-diagnosis-245749

18. http://www.calmclinic.com/anxiety/christian-relationship-in-overcoming-anxiety

19. http://www.adaa.org/understanding-anxiety/related-illnesses/bipolar-disorder-2

20. http://psycheducation.org/the-biologic-basis-of-bipolar-disorder/

21. http://psycheducation.org/diagnosis/mixed-states/anxiety-and-bipolar-disorder/

22. http://mentalhealthdaily.com/2015/02/26/5-new-anxiety-medications-in-development-2015/

23. http://bipolar.stanford.edu/patient.html

24. https://www.nami.org/Learn-More/Treatment/Mental-Health-Medications/Olanzapine-(Zyprexa)

25. http://www.webmd.com/bipolar-disorder/guide/bipolar-2-disorder

26. http://www.healthline.com/health/bipolar-disorder/history-bipolar#4

27. https://www.sciencedaily.com/news/mind_brain/bipolar_disorder/

28. http://www.bphope.com/blog/when-living-with-bipolar-disorder-changes-your-life/

29. http://neurocritic.blogspot.com/2013/08/breakthroughs-in-bipolar-treatment.html